Gallery Sound

ex:centrics

Series Editors:

Greg Hainge and Paul Hegarty

Gallery Sound

Caleb Kelly

Bloomsbury Academic
An imprint of Bloomsbury Publishing Inc

B L O O M S B U R Y

NEW YORK • LONDON • OXFORD • NEW DELHI • SYDNEY

Bloomsbury Academic
An imprint of Bloomsbury Publishing Inc

1385 Broadway
New York
NY 10018
USA

50 Bedford Square
London
WC1B 3DP
UK

www.bloomsbury.com

BLOOMSBURY and the Diana logo are trademarks of Bloomsbury Publishing Plc

First published 2017

Library of Congress Cataloging-in-Publication Data:
Names: Kelly, Caleb, 1972- author.
Title: Gallery sound / Caleb Kelly.
Description: New York: Bloomsbury Academic, 2017. | Series: Ex:centrics | Includes bibliographical references and index.
Identifiers: LCCN 2016058527 (print) | LCCN 2016058950 (ebook) | ISBN 9781501304378 (hardback: alk. paper) | ISBN 9781501304361 (pbk.: alk. paper) | ISBN 9781501304385 (ePDF) | ISBN 9781501304392 (ePUB)
Subjects: LCSH: Sound in art. | Sound installations (Art) | Art museums.
Classification: LCC NX650.S68 K45 2017 (print) | LCC NX650.S68 (ebook) | DDC 709.04/074–dc23
LC record available at https://lccn.loc.gov/2016058527]

ISBN: HB: 978-1-5013-0437-8
PB: 978-1-5013-0436-1
ePDF: 978-1-5013-0438-5
ePub: 978-1-5013-0439-2

Series: ex:centrics

Cover image ©: Kusum Normoyle in performance for the opening of Sound Full (2012) in front of Marco Fusinato, Reproduction of *Double Infinitive 2* (2012). Courtesy of the artist. Photograph Brodie Thompon

Typeset by Deanta Global Publishing Services, Chennai, India
Printed and bound in the United States of America

CONTENTS

ACKNOWLEDGEMENTS

The research process as a whole and the development of ideas into this book developed out of a surprising series of twists and turns, dead ends and moments of unexpected joy. I have spent the last twenty years with my head deep in sound in art and music; it saturates my workday and my spare time. This book is a product of having sonic interest in the arts both as an academic and as an event producer/curator who has extensively exploited the gallery space as a site for the production of soundful happenings. Within these various practices the gallery has taken numerous forms, from artist-run spaces to art museums and the events themselves are numerous in type from noise music festivals to biennale events, all has taught me something about sound within the gallery.

More specifically the book has had a rather long gestation; back in 2010 it first surfaced as an attempted Australian Research Council grant application. It was with some surprise that the editors of the ex:centrics series a few years later invited me to propose a book that was very similar in scope to my initial proposal. I was delighted to write the book and so thanks needs to be directed to Greg Hainge and Paul Hegarty for having faith in this book project.

Douglas Kahn needs to be acknowledged and thanked here. I've known him since he was my PhD supervisor around the turn of the century and he has been my mentor ever since. From the days of being his student to the year I was his boss to now a colleague at UNSW in Sydney where we work together on the Sound, Energies and Environments Research Group within NIEA, Doug continues to be an inspiration.

The second individual thank you goes to Peter Blamey who has officially worked on this project as an editor and who has been a sounding board and a font of truth throughout the writing of it. Our conversations about art and music have helped shape this book in many many ways.

An extended period of research and writing was conducted while I was the Edgard Varèse Guest Professor at the Technische Universität Berlin and the DAAD. I resided in Berlin for four months in 2015 and experienced many works that I would otherwise not have witnessed.

I would also like to thank Maria Müller-Schareck who granted me access to the Konrad Fischer Galerie archive housed at Kunstsammlung NRW in Düsseldorf. A morning spent rummaging through the correspondence between Nauman and his gallerist was enlightening to say the least.

I would like to acknowledge an extended period of resilience from my faculty at UNSW: Art & Design, from which I have been granted periods of research during numerous international trips while writing this book, as well as a publishing grant from the faculty. I would specifically thank the dean, Ross Harley in this regard.

The editors from my past books need mention: Roger Conover at MIT Press and Ian Farr who edits the wonderful Documents of Contemporary Art series with Whitechapel Gallery and MIT Press. These publications continue to open doors for me and for that I am extremely grateful.

Many colleagues, friends and family have helped along the way, whether directly in conversation, by allowing me to publicly try out parts of the book, or by providing inspiration:

Marco Fusinato, Brent Grayburn, Honor Harger, Bella Star, Aki Onda, Seth Cluett, Joel Stern, Atau Tanaka, Ellen Rutten, Yngvar Steinholt, Steven Connor, Teresa Dillon, Charles Eppley, Seth Kim-Cohen, Jasmine Guffond, Ari Benjamin Meyers, Marina Rosenfeld, Angelica Mesiti, David Haines, Joyce Hinterding, Branden Joseph, Tom Apperley, Frances Dyson, Christof Migone, Kusum Normoyle, Brandon LaBelle, Hong-Kai Wang, Vicky Browne, Marley Dawson, Bree Pickering, Aaron Kreisler, Anna Munster, Lara Bown, Michael Hodgeson, Uroš Čvoro, Justin Luke, LoVid (Tali and Kyle), Ross Gibson, Astrid Lorange, Christine Ross, Melle Kromhout and Belinda J Dunstan.

I acknowledge my current PhD students who, while sharing my research interests, continually remind me of the writing process and the many many reasons to research: Andrew Brookes, Nathan Thompson, Vincent O'Connor, Tom Smith and Justin Harvey.

Lastly I want to thank Lynn Kelly, the mother of my son Jarvis, who has put up with numerous research trips throughout the course of writing this book. And of course Jarvis who, although only nine and still not understanding how I am a 'doctor', has helpfully explained that I am a doctor who helps people who are sick of art.

Introduction

Australian artist Marco Fusinato's installation *Constellations* (2015) at the Institute of Contemporary Art, Singapore, is an extraordinary installation, largely because it could potentially be the loudest work ever installed in an art gallery. The gallery itself is typical in that it has long white walls, a polished concrete floor and industrial ceiling fittings. Clean, white and empty, for the most part the only discernible sound within the space is the clicking footsteps of patrons. A 46-metre-long wall bisects the expansive exhibition space. The wall has been beautifully constructed and looks as if it is a permanent fixture. Attached to the wall is a long metal chain connected to a baseball bat, the only visible object present within the gallery. The audience for *Constellations* is tasked with striking the wall with the bat, a rather strange thing to expect anyone to do. As could be expected from an artist so inextricably linked to noise, there is a catch to the violent thump of bat on wall; the strike causes 120 decibels of sound to blast out from inside the wall. The sound is on the pain threshold and is louder than most rock concerts and the equivalent to that of a chainsaw.

When the exhibition began, the wall was pristine, but by the end of the exhibition it had been severely damaged with large chunks now 'missing' and chipped paint hanging off its surface. In documentation of the installation people can be seen with bat in hand, throwing themselves at the wall, hitting it as hard as they can (so much so that a rule of one hit per person was eventually introduced). In fact, in the first days of the exhibition four wooden baseball bats were snapped, causing the artist to replace them with an aluminium bat. There is something quite peculiar in the act of striking the gallery wall, the apparent strangeness and humour in the action is met with a brutal torrent of white noise that is both terrifying and comical. The sound generated by the strike intervenes in the expected norms of gallery conduct and in the unspoken expectation for quiet within the art institution.

The audio produced from the clout emanates from a sizeable sound system installed within the wall. Contact microphones were placed around the strike zone such that when the bat made contact with the wall, the microphones would pick up the sound produced, sending the signal to the sound system where they were massively amplified. The work cannot help but raise ethical issues around the health and safety of those subjected to the torrent of sound. The installation has drawn questions in public talks I have given of how a work this loud, possibly dangerously loud, could be presented in a public environment? Interestingly the exhibition did not generate a single noise complaint and many audience members returned numerous times, for instance to let off steam between classes (the gallery being located within an art school). In general, far quieter sounds within the bounds of other art galleries have drawn complaints in the past, but not the sonic blasts generated by *Constellations*.

Constellations makes use of the gallery architecture to its fullest. The hard floors, flat walls and all but empty space are palpably filled, albeit for brief moments at a time, with sound pressure and reverberating air. If this was not enough, the installation room's 'noise floor' (the sum of all noise sources within a system, here the gallery) was dramatically heightened for a full day when Fusinato performed a six-hour version of his guitar noise performance work *Spectral Arrows*. The art museum installed a disproportionately large sound system, including two bass guitar amps, alongside a sound system that would fill a concert venue with audio. With only a relatively small number of visitors in the gallery at any one time over the course of the performance, sound was not dampened by the bodies of the audience as would occur with larger numbers in attendance. Thus sound ricocheted around the room, reinforcing itself and raising the air pressure even further. The reverberation within the gallery was consequently extreme, causing Fusinato's thick and multilayered noise music to fold in on itself over an extended duration.

a Listening to visual art

Sounds fill the gallery spaces of the art world. Upon entering almost any contemporary gallery space, we hear sound emanating from TV monitors, projection spaces, computers and in headphones, alongside the daily sounds made by gallery staff, art patrons, the gallery bookshop and so on. The gallery is not the hushed space it was once imagined to be, but filled with noisy, quiet, disruptive, overlapping, discrepant, loud, brutal, pretty, aggressive and/ or harmonious sounds. This is not unproblematic as the hard, square surfaces of the gallery do not manage sound well; instead of remaining localized, sounds are reflected all around the space, bumping into other sounds that have crept out of adjoining galleries and interfering with each other in the process. In addition, many contemporary practices stage the gallery as a social space, somewhere we have conversations, eat, drink and participate. Well-known examples of such practices include Rirkrit Tiravanija's *untitled (free)* (1992) in which participants ate rice and Thai curry cooked by the artist, and Olafur Eliasson's *The Weather Project* (2003) installed in the Tate Modern's Turbine Hall for which visitors attended numerous times creating a social space within the art museum.

To begin with, compare two very different environments employed for the display of audiovisual work: the cinematic theatre and the art gallery. The former is dark, plush and comfortable; the latter is white, stark and unforgiving. Andrew Uroskie, in his book *Between the Black Box and the White Cube*, details the differences: 'Within the gallery's brightly illuminated container, the aesthetic spectator navigates a physical encounter with the space of the object-come-installation in a temporality of their choosing. The cinema's box, by contrast, intentionally negates both bodily mobility and environmental perception so as to transport the viewer *away* from her present time and local space' (Uroskie 2014, 5).

The contemporary cinema was created for viewing moving images and listening to highly produced audio, while the gallery space was created for viewing visual art. The cinema attempts to lull us into forgetting our physical presence in the theatre, while the art gallery constantly alerts us to the fact that we are looking at art and that we are present. The venues for film and contemporary art have a relatively short history, but the rationale behind these architectures demonstrates an approach that was very different from what was originally envisaged to be presented within these spaces.

Art was not always presented single file in stark white galleries; not very long ago, pictures were stacked high on the wall in the grand salons across Europe. However, in the last century or so, art has become singular, requiring space and an environment that is cleaned of visual impairment. There is a strong desire for an uninterrupted line of sight and, as a result, the white cube is the cleanest and most obvious choice. In this logic, sound was simply not conceived as a condition of these visual art spaces. Steven Connor, a historian of sound, voice and auditory media, in his essay 'Ears Have Walls', points to the difficulty of exhibiting sound in galleries, arguing that galleries have been formed to highlight visuality, their sharp angles designed for visual rather than sonic containment: 'Sound work makes us aware of the continuing emphasis upon division and partition that continues to exist even in the most radically revisable or polymorphous gallery space, because sound spreads and leaks, like odour' (Connor 2011, 129).

The harsh, hard surfaces of the gallery ignore the multitude of technologies designed over the last century to curb the diffusion of sound. In her book *The Soundscape of Modernity*, Emily Thompson, a historian of technology, highlights the radical transformation of our sonic environments, beginning in the early part of the twentieth century, which were shaped by scientific methods for controlling sound. Thompson attests, 'A fundamental compulsion to control the behaviour of sound drove technological developments in architectural acoustics' (Thompson 2002, 2), for example, by changing the reverberation time of a room by curbing the way sound moved through a given space. Thompson's argument is that sound was controlled and shaped in a technologically driven and modernist manner, most distinctly within the developing cinema theatres, while elements of sound behaviour such as reverberation were removed altogether. Next time you are at the cinema take note of how this practice continues to form our movie-going experience. The soft coverings on the floors, walls and chairs are there to dampen the sound by lessening sound reflection. In addition to rendering the space as a listening capsule, cinema developed playback technologies such as 5.1 surround sound that creates an immersive sound, further suturing us into the cinematic experience. As we will see in the following pages, this is radically different from the gestation of the art gallery and its development into the white-walled container of contemporary art.

Gallery Sound has its gestation within my history as an event producer and curator who has extensively employed the art gallery as a venue for exhibition and for the performance of music. The ideas found in this book were originally generated within a practice that sought to utilize a problematic architecture and interior design to promote soundful arts practices. However, this book is not about the inherent problems or issues with curating within the art gallery; this is definitely not a how-to manual. Rather this is a book that listens back to the gallery space, hearing afresh an environment that is always already brimming with sonic artefacts, a space that is never silent.

In the early 1950s, American experimental composer John Cage argued explicitly for the impossibility of silence, arguing that 'silence is all of the sound we don't intend', and 'there is no such thing as absolute silence' (Kahn 1999, 163). Cage created a piece of very noisy silence entitled *4′33″* (1952) in the process of considering this impossibility of absolute silence. The work at first might seem to be about silence since the performer of the piece sits silently without playing a note on their instrument for the duration of the piece. For the premiere it was David Tudor in front of a grand piano, but in fact the composition actually frames listening and all the sounds that occur during its performance. What is garnered from listening to the piece is that silence is anything but silent and that within the time frame of the performance all manner of sounds can be heard. For Douglas Kahn, a historian of the sounding arts, *4′33″* was the 'ultimate *silent piece*' (italics in original), which 'could occur anywhere and anytime, all sounds could be music, and no one need to make music for music to exist' (163).

If sound is ever present, then it follows from this that art galleries contain sound and therefore are never silent. Sound is present in the gallery in numerous ways, whether in everyday sounds, in incidental or deliberate sound, in extremely loud or imperceptibly quiet sounds, or in the conversations and imagination of the audience. It is crucial in reading *Gallery Sound* that the reader understands that I am taking Cage at his word: that there really is no such thing as silence, not in a landscape painting, not in a marble sculpture and certainly not in an art gallery. Artworks already and always come with and are immersed in sound. The architecture of the gallery is filled with sounds, images fill our minds with sound, the acoustic space of the gallery is transformed by installations and sometimes works produce sounds themselves. By listening closely to the sounds of the art gallery, both literally and in our imagination, from within the art and incidentally to the art, we will comprehend art in a richer and fuller manner, one that can take into account the full spectrum of our human perception.[1]

Silence, it would seem, can never be silent. A series of installations of not quite silent silences was installed at Temple Contemporary in Philadelphia (curated by Robert Blackson). For this series artists were commissioned to produce a work that responded to a particular kind of silence. For this series Ann Hamilton, Sophie Calle, Autumn Chacon and Cornelia Parker were commissioned to produce works that 'alter the assumed silence of the gallery by adding additional layers of commissioned silences to the space' (Blackson 2016). Sophie Calle worked with the silence that occurred for five minutes across the entire Domino's Pizza chain in America during the OJ Simpson trial verdict, during which time not a single pizza was ordered throughout the chain in the United States. To register this (non)event, she recorded her silence in an actual Domino's Pizza kitchen. Cornelia Parker's silence, entitled *Sitting Thinking About Explosions in a Small Quiet Room* (2012), is a recording of her doing just that. This work has itself been released as a record on which is recorded the sounds in the room in which Parker was sitting while thinking about the extremely loud sounds of explosions. Parker is most well known for her installations such as *Cold Dark Matter: An Exploded View* (1991) that halt time in the course of an explosion by suspending objects in space. The artist's imagining of explosions can then be heard within the frame of a 'sonic imagination' that continues her investigation of very loud moments in time.

These performances of silence that played silently into the art gallery are a reflection on the assumed quietude of the exhibition environment on the one hand and the expectation that a sounding work is not silent on the other. The installations hardly affected the gallery environment, playing well below the noise floor and deliberately attracting very little attention, silently going about their performance in the background of the louder regular programmed exhibitions.

There is a complex relationship to silence within the setting of the art gallery that bumps up against the impossibility of actual silence within any environment. The quietest places on earth are those located within the architectural structures known as anechoic chambers, with Microsoft's chamber at Redmond in Washington being the quietest. This research facility has officially recorded decibel levels of –20.6 dB (the theoretically quietest possible measurement being –23 dB) (Microsoft 2015). As will be discussed later, the anechoic chamber has been influential on artists interested in experiential practices and it was a key driver in the development of John Cage's thinking about silence and it was a technology later used by American artists Robert Irwin and James Turrell to create sensory deprivation that caused those inside to experience their sense of hearing in a heightened manner. In the hands of these artists the lack of sensory experience becomes the art itself, shifting so-called visual art into the realms of the senses.

I could include here numerous quotations that point to an insufficient understanding of sound as it pertains to visual art. To take but one example from 2015: 'Sound installation remains under-recognized within historical accounts of twentieth-century art and music' (Ouzounian 2015, 73), writes Gascia Ouzounian, a musicologist and sound artist, but many similar claims are repeated regularly in contemporary literature focused on sound. As far back as 1990, Kahn named the twentieth century 'the deaf century' (Kahn 1990), pointing to a history of art investigation that almost completely negated sound as a component of so-called 'visual art'. At this stage in the burgeoning disciplines of sound research we have most likely reached a point where these types of statements should no longer be necessary, but sound remains a concern within art discourses because it continues to be insufficiently acknowledged and theorized within the realm of the so-called visual arts. Sound in art is too often, as the above quotation suggests, under-recognized, but even when it is recognized this is often done inadvertently. For example, many reviews and discussions of the work of Dan Flavin discuss the electrical sound produced by his fluorescent lights, and it is a fact that his works produce a constant electrical buzz. Yet Flavin is never called a sound artist and his works are not discussed as sound installation even if they are regularly discussed in relation to the sound they produce. This is critical to the logic of this book, a point of departure that is generative rather than a point of negation. That is, we do not need to create a special category for sound in art as it is always and forever present. What we do need to do is to become more aware of the environment in which art is displayed and the simple fact that we perceive our art, and the world in which we are in, through all of our senses.

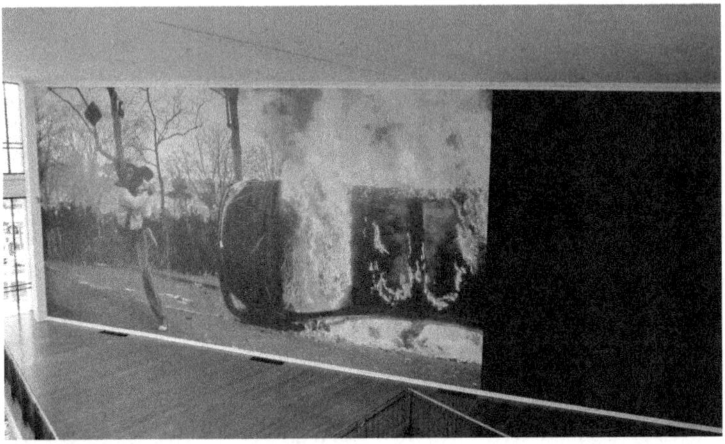

FIGURE 1 Marco Fusinato, *Reproduction of Double Infinitive* 2 (2012), installation view, *Sound Full*, Dunedin Public Art Gallery, New Zealand. Courtesy of the artist, Anna Schwartz Gallery.

In 2012 I curated an exhibition for the Dunedin Public Art Gallery, a large art museum for a small city at the tail end of New Zealand and additionally the city in which I grew up. The exhibition entitled Sound Full: Sound in Contemporary Australian and New Zealand Art featured works by thirteen artists, all of whom employed or investigated sound as an aspect of their work. Marco Fusinato was offered a very large wall that overlooks the entrance way from above. The wall is some 24 metres long and 7 metres high. He suggested we produce a version of his work *Double Infinitives* to completely cover the wall.

Double Infinitives is a series of works originally produced in 2009 that take street riots as their subject. The images were sourced from newspapers following a series of rules, requiring that the artist use 'a selection of images from the print media of the decisive moment in a riot in which a protagonist brandishes a rock against a backdrop of fire. Each image is from a different part of the world, from the early twenty-first century, and is blown up to history-painting scale using the latest commercial print technologies' (Fusinato 2009).

Once the images were sourced, they were originally blown up in size to 250 × 625 cm. At this scale they are approximately human size and when I first saw them hung in a very quiet white art gallery, I found these images to be filled with an imaginary sound to the point of noisiness. When further enlarged to the size of the gigantic wall they become extremely noisy. The original newspaper image sourced by Fusinato is printed in halftone, a process that uses dots to reproduce photographs, meaning that when scaled up to mural scale for Sound Full the black and white circles become visible – so visible that when up close the image ceases to be recognizable. Standing at a distance the work crowds the space in black and white noise. This printing process is very noisy in terms of its resolution as the process is far from a high-resolution printing process and a lot of information is thus lost. It is instructive to look at these works reprinted with people standing in front. In particular, there is an image of the wallpaper hanger installing the work in Dunedin. The image was printed in a newspaper so was itself printed in halftone, making it look as though the workman was actually brushing directly onto a burning vehicle.

The mural-sized work, entitled *Reproduction of Double Infinitive 2* (2012), is also excessively noisy in terms of its content; it is so loud that it fills the space with a deafening noise! While the work does not contain audio, our sonic imagination hears this image and its abundance of sound. A violent and raucous scene of a crowd gathered to riot (against what we do not know) is pictured.[2] A car has been

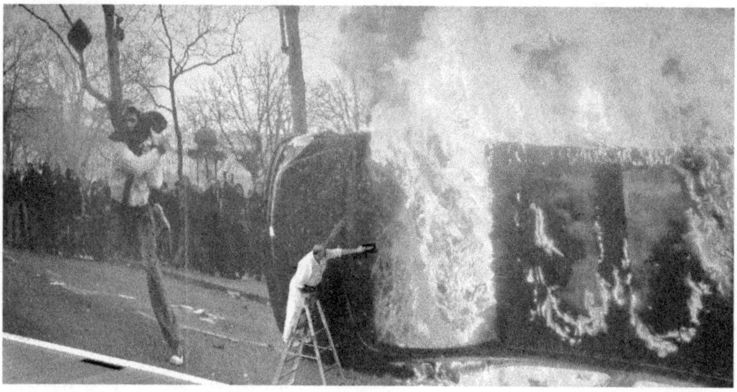

FIGURE 2 Installation of Marco Fusinato, *Reproduction of Double Infinitive 2* (2012), *Sound Full*, Dunedin Public Art Gallery, New Zealand: Photograph: Otago Daily Times.

rolled over and set on fire and a figure on the far left has just thrown a rock that is photographed mid-trajectory. I argue that we cannot look at this image without imagining the sounds associated with the riot, the yelling people and the crackling of the burning car. It is here that the 'sonic imagination' takes place. The viewer of any figurative artwork imagines in some way what they witness within an image. When we see a picturesque landscape painting, we imagine the farm animals, the smell of the grass and the sounds of the birds. We do not imagine the scene through only one sense, that is, as a purely visual spectacle – the scene after all is not purely visual. Just as we experience the world through multiple senses, so too do we remember and locate visual images through our full bodily, multisensory experience. Thus, the imagined sonic experience of *Reproduction of Double Infinitive 2*, an apparently soundless work, was excessive and deafening.

A key element of hearing this work is an understanding of Cage's dictum: there is no such thing as silence. The work does not have audio of any kind associated with it; there are no speakers in this work, yet here I am describing it as being filled with sound. However, in his catalogue essay 'Dark Energy: The Art of Marco Fusinato', art historian Branden Joseph states of the work: 'Fusinato's piece remained starkly and impassively silent' (2014, 199). This is an instance of an art historian reading an artwork by only accounting for the visual (or even visible) factors of the work despite there being many cues within the work itself to indicate that in fact it has a sounding element to it. An art historian looks at an image or, as Joseph describes this work, a picture, and sees its content (imagining the image to represent something visual), but more often than not they do not imagine its sonic content. This would be to conceive of a world in which, for example, we can recall what something looked like, something we saw in the past, but where we cannot evoke what something sounded like, something we heard in the past.

Why then does an art historian focus solely on the visual aspects of a work without imagining its sonic qualities, 'seeing' the event represented in the image but not 'hearing' it? I put 'see' in scare quotes because when I look at an image of a man throwing a paving stone I clearly do not see an actual person throwing a paving stone, I see (in this case) some rather large dots that form the shape of a person, but certainly not a person as such. It might also mean that, in the art historian's mind, they imagine the person they are seeing represented as one-dimensional, as consisting only of visuality. That is, they do not imagine their presence or vantage point to be that of the photographer at the time when the original photograph was taken. Yet if we were able to take up the position of the photographer we would of course be in the position of perceiving the events before us aurally as well as visually. In addition, we would hear the fire blazing in front of us, smell the burning car and feel the heat emanating from it, and taste the smoke in the air.

Joseph's reading of Fusinato's practice is predominantly cultural/political in approach, and it is the case that Fusinato's work is always a political act, but what such an understanding of his practice misses is that whether there is audio present or not, his interventionist approach to installation within the art museum is bound up in our expectations of the proper and correct manner in which sound is employed in the gallery. In this case the artist has installed a massive non-sounding mural in an exhibition explicitly directed towards the sound arts. Much like Christian Marclay, who engages sound and music with reference to popular (music) culture, Fusinato is a contemporary artist who utilizes a variety of media to produce a gallery practice in which sound is never an end in itself (sound in itself, so to speak). Rather, sound is a powerful tool that runs through all of his work, indicating 'an interest in the intensity of a gesture or event' (Joseph 2014, 195).

While the previous example was mobilized as an exemplar of the sonic imagination, other key experiences of sound in the gallery setting relate directly to the physical attributes of spaces. These acoustic properties are subject to being modified or transformed to such an extent that we are made highly aware of the sonic environment of the gallery and the sound experiences we might have within it. The installation *Telepathy* (2008) by Australian media artists David Haines and Joyce Hinterding is a case in point. A large yellow free-standing triangular structure was installed in a massive gallery space within an old train construction facility in Sydney. On the day that I visited the exhibition my 4-year-old son accompanied me. The yellow structure contains an intensely sound-dampened interior constructed from purpose-built anechoic acoustic tiles so as to stop outside sounds from entering. When shut inside the space the audience is sonically cut off from the outside gallery and any sounds they make are not reflected, creating a sense of extreme isolation. While inside I made a number of sounds (handclaps and vocal noises) in order to gauge my son's reaction, but as it turns out he did not pay the lack of sound reflection any attention whatsoever. On exiting *Telepathy*, we re-entered what was a highly reflective gallery space, effectively a massive reverberation chamber, the polar opposite to the inside of the work. Once outside, my son heard the reverberation of the gallery and began to make very loud shouts and squeals, loving the sound of his voice being reflected throughout the gallery. The work demonstrated to us a difference between the unreflective and acoustically dampened space and the highly reflective and reverberant gallery. It was the contrast between the acoustical properties of the two divergent spaces that made me and my son strongly aware of the room sounds.

Most of the examples I have discussed so far are known to me through experience: I did attend Haines and Hinterding's installation and I did strike the gallery wall with a baseball bat in Fusinato's *Constellations* exhibition. *Gallery Sound* takes as its point of departure an experience of art and music that is embodied, attesting to the multi-sensory experience of the arts. In terms of research methodology, I have attended many of the works that will be discussed within the book (at least the contemporary ones) and as such I can attest to their sounding and my understanding of them through my own lived experience. This cannot always be the case, however, and I have not, for the most part, experienced the works examined in the next section, entitled 'The Empty-sounding Gallery', for the simple reason that I was not alive in 1969. As I have not been able to be in attendance at these events, as is common in historical research, I have been required to come to know of these practices and examples through the historical record – archives, reviews, articles and subsequent critical attention that has been paid to the works by scholars. By employing a scholarly method that relies on the historical record I am indebted to those who were in attendance to document their own experience. The majority of the documentation that exists is in the form of written text and photographic evidence with very little sound recording being available. If, as I will argue, sound has not been the focus of this attention, however, then there arises an issue in relation to the possibility of knowing these works as aurally experienced practices.

The written word and the photograph are the main historical records we utilize in the scholarship of art and I wish to argue here that a key reason for the lack of attention paid to sound within the history of art is due to the photographic documentation of artworks. Words only document and describe what is seen and heard through language, which is never a substitute for lived experience. However, it can certainly be argued that sound has been written about in accounts of exhibitions, and that these accounts of the aural experience of art have the same positive and negative issues as those of a discussion of the visual experience of art. That said, the written record of non-visual experience suffers from the lack of attention paid to it due to an overwhelming focus on visuality. If the author of a review, for example, is solely focused on writing about visual art, we cannot get a sense of the aural experience of that reviewer.

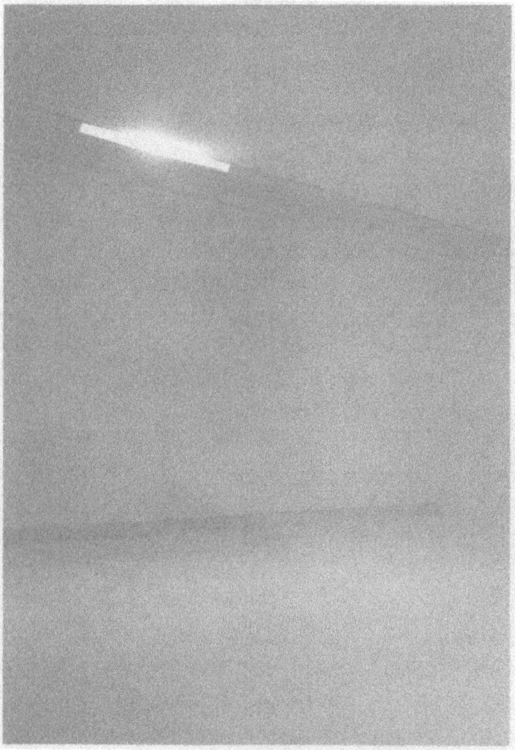

FIGURE 3 Michael Asher, La Jolla Museum of Art, La Jolla, California, U.S.A., November 7–December 31, 1969, northwest corner of constructed wall and existing wall. © Michael Asher Foundation

I have long been struck by the documentation of Michael Asher's exhibition at La Jolla Museum of Art in 1969. The empty gallery presented by Asher created an environment that rendered the audience highly aware of their spatial presence through the manipulation of the acoustic properties of the gallery with the addition of a sine tone. The photographs of the installation can represent neither the aural sensory space produced nor the audio component of the installation. In fact, when we look at this documentation, all that we see is a rather blurry image of a white space. My argument, in essence, is that this long-habituated practice of art and exhibition documentation has established a cause-and-effect relation between the way in which art is experienced even within the gallery space at the time of exhibition. To put this another way, if our predominant mode of documentation of art is visual, and in most cases we come to know of artworks and exhibitions through photographs, then this comes to condition the ways that we understand, conceptualize and discuss artworks. Unless we were actually present at La Jolla Art Museum, we cannot possibly determine from the photographic evidence what it sounded like. Thus our understanding of art continues to reside primarily in the visual, even within contemporary art practices that are predominantly multimodal.

There is no doubt that the record of historic exhibitions has been documented visually, through the use of the photograph. Art books, magazines and newspaper reviews are furnished with photographs that serve to show the artworks and exhibitions (often in situ) being discussed in art history and art criticism. These singular photographic documents do not represent the spatial aspect of many installations, nor do they document any time-based element of the work. While video documentation does exist, it is rarely included in any published text (although this was briefly experimented with by including CD or DVD documentation within books that focused primarily on time-based media). There have also been practices of publication that link the reader directly to websites and online documentation, but this is an unpopular and rather clunky approach. In what follows, however, I am not so much interested in the discussion of publishing practices and alternative methods of presenting documentation; rather, the point I wish to make is that, in the overwhelming majority of cases, the record of an exhibition, whether purely visual and object-based, or installation and time-based, is represented in photographs.

For quite some time I have been thinking about sound in art documentation. As historians of the arts we are accustomed to looking at photographic documentation of artworks, exhibitions, installations and performances. Academically we learn the 'visual analysis' of artworks, and we look at the historical record and read artworks from their documentation. What we cannot do from photographs is hear the artwork. We can, as argued above, imagine the sounds if the visual aspects of the exhibition are tightly connected to the sonic elements, or, if we have actually experienced the exhibition, the photographic documentation might be enough to jog our memory of how it sounded. The real issue occurs when the photograph does not elucidate any sound aspect of the exhibition. For example, we cannot hear the sound of Asher's sine tone nor can we hear the room's acoustics (is the room bright and loud or dull and quiet?). I believe this has led to the negative attitudes that abound around a lack of skill and knowledge in how to analyse artworks in terms of sound. I have heard perfectly able academics tell me they are not 'sound people', evidence of an unwillingness to engage with any perceivable aspects of art beyond the visual. Yet we are all sound people, alongside taste people, smell people and touch people.[3]

b A sound context

In the last decade 'sound studies' has become a field of research that has produced numerous publications, including monographs, readers, dedicated journals and conferences. Sound studies, in the broadest sense of the term, could well be used to situate this book, but I am inclined to remain on the edge of this emergent field. In part this comes from many years of being just on the outside of cultural studies, popular music studies, visual cultures and most recently sound studies. While my research crosses into areas covered by these fields of enquiry, it does not make for a comfortable fit. In 2014 I was asked to be part of a plenary for a literary studies conference entitled *Modern Soundscapes* alongside Steven Connor and Bruce Johnson. During the conference I had been struck by how little was being said that was actually about sound. Rather, the focus of the majority of papers was on the cultures that surrounded various sounds. I responded to this observation during the panel by questioning the actual interest in sound itself, rather than the cultural and social effects of sound. Were the presenters actually interested in the effects of sound or was sound merely an emerging area that could be harnessed to further already existent discourses in the field of literary studies? That is, was this merely the performance of a fashionable moment?[4]

A year after the plenary, Connor gave the closing address at the *Sound Studies: Art, Experience, Politics* conference, stating:

> One might imagine that sound studies ought simply and straightforwardly to be concerned with the investigation of sound phenomena and experiences. ... Sound studies have not been pursued simply because there is sound, or because sound is just there. For many of those who pursue it, and who are pursued by it, the study of sound is part of a larger project or programme, which is aimed, not just at expanding what we know about sound, but changing the nature of knowledge about everything and the manner we have of acquiring it. Many of those who have made the most decisive contributions to the understanding of sound have done so on the basis of an intense idealisation of sound experience, and a kind of onerous dream, mad as it may seem. (2015)

This 'mad dream' is one in which visual dominance is replaced with an aural dominance. This is certainly not my plan for this book. I am not calling for the deliberate replacement of visual art with aural art, nor am I going to argue that listening to an artwork is somehow more virtuous than viewing it. Sound studies scholar Jonathan Sterne points to what he names the 'audiovisual litany' that, 'idealizes hearing as manifesting a kind of pure interiority. It alternately denigrates and elevates vision: as a fallen sense, vision takes us out of the world' (2003, 15).

An over-identification with the aural is just as problematic as it is in the realm of the visual. Musicologist Nina Sun Eidsheim begins her book *Sensing Sound* with an interesting take on the conundrum, 'If a tree falls in the forest and no one is there to hear it, does it make a sound?' She asks us to imagine actually being where the tree is falling, stating, 'The sound of the falling tree might be one of your lesser concerns' (Eidsheim 2015, 1). She imagines all of the other effects caused by a nearby falling tree, such as the sounds made by birds fleeing the event, dust raised by the tree thumping into the ground causing stinging eyes and a dry throat, and the thump of the tree crashing into the earth vibrating your body. Alerting us to Clifford Geertz's ethnographic sense of a 'thick description', Eidsheim reasons, 'Interpreting a sense experience in terms of just one of the physical senses cannot take full account of the event's complexities' (1). Aiming her critique at sound and music, she states that music relies so strongly on the figure of sound that it limits our ability to experience it (7). Here I would argue that similar problems occur within visual art. Its very naming as *visual* limits the experience of an artwork to the visual sense and shields us from engaging other senses when in its presence.

I am sure it could be argued that contemporary art commonly engages other senses in forms such as installation work, time-based practices, performance art and video art, and as such we have become familiar with a multi-sensory experience of art. While this might be the case in specific contemporary-leaning art galleries, it is certainly not the case in more traditional settings such as art museums. Within this context, a sounding artwork can cause all sorts of issues for the curator, docents, invigilators, security guards and the audience. Imagine trying to quietly contemplate a Picasso or Cezanne painting while recorded sound bleeds from a nearby gallery! Yet it is my argument that we always approach art with a thick employment of the senses, from within our bodies. It is then the mechanisms of the art institution that continually direct us to think about art visually; as visual art.

Throughout the book a number of terms to describe exhibition spaces will recur. While I do not want to completely lock down these terms, it is important to delineate the differences between them. The term 'gallery' is used to describe any space of exhibition and is employed across the various strata of exhibition spaces including very small alternative galleries, commercial galleries, art centres and museums. These galleries can be single spaces; the whole art gallery can be one exhibition space or form a part of a series of exhibition spaces. An 'art museum' is something more specific in that there is a requirement that the institution hold a collection, thus an art museum is usually understood to be a peak body of the institution of art. While there is some confusion over naming conventions, for example the major art museum in Sydney is called the Art Gallery of New South Wales, for my own purposes art museums are institutional spaces that collect art.

The context for this book is the art gallery and it is my contention that this context itself generates practice. I do not mean that everything that is placed in an art gallery is somehow affected by the specifics of this containment – the coffee in the gallery café is no different from the coffee in a corner café and the string quartet performing in the background of a gala function held within the art gallery is no different from what they perform at a wedding. However, as will be demonstrated, there are many examples of practices that rely on these spaces to produce works that are contingent on the specifics of gallery architecture.

The gallery walls are white of course. The floor is white, grey or brown depending on whether it is painted, polished concrete or wood. The ceiling is white and dotted with lights directed at the wall or lined with fluorescent tubes. There are rarely any windows. Between exhibitions the walls are repainted or touched up (and at times moved), bringing them back to a state of purity. At that moment the white cube is at its most pristine; it has no marks, no scuffs and no art within its hard edges, giving the illusion of a cultural rebirthing of the space, of a permanently renewed innocence. Sound, it can be argued, is never of itself but rather is formed and known from within various cultures and historical periods – as such, sound is never innocent. This is certainly the case for the examples that will be discussed in this book. Sound is formed within the gallery, within ideologies of art practices and within the bounds of social pressures, and sound is framed by expectations and social norms when it enters the art institution. The examples discussed in *Gallery Sound* are most often in excess of these norms: either they hush the space beyond the well-mannered quietude of the art gallery or they intervene with explosive noise when least expected, breaking all bounds of respectful sound.

The so-called 'white cube' gallery is ubiquitous, to the point where white hard walls are considered the 'natural' space for the display of artworks. Of course the interior of the gallery did not develop naturally but is embedded deeply with cultural expectations and modernist ideologies. German art historian Charlotte Klonk, in her history of the development of exhibition spaces in the early to mid-twentieth century, aligns what she names the 'white flexible art container' with the first decade of the Museum of Modern Art (MoMA) in New York, and its inaugural director Alfred H. Barr. Discussing the first exhibition of 1931, which was held in an office space, Klonk states: 'The fact that he hung the pictures intimately and at a somewhat lower height than usual shows that Barr still followed the conception of gallery-going as a private, interiorised experience that had emerged in Germany around 1900' (2009, 138). Klonk goes on to explain that Barr later in 1936 had arrived at a definitive mode of display, 'the white "neutral" container that permitted a flexible arrangement of the work on show and offered the visitor a calm, yet dynamic viewing experience' (138).[5]

Brian O'Doherty influentially critiqued the 'white cube' in a series of three articles published in *Artforum* in 1976, which describe the modernist ideology and context in which the architecture of the gallery space developed. The white cube serves to frame an artwork that is believed to be timeless and eternal, allowing the pieces to be removed from the derogating dirtiness of the everyday, to be placed in an apolitical space that is 'limbo-like'. Key to his argument is his observation that the art gallery isolates the artwork 'from everything that would detract from its own evaluation of itself' (O'Doherty 1999, 14). The gallery is designed to allow art total separation from the everyday, cutting off the exhibition spaces from the outside: 'Walls are painted white. The ceiling becomes the source of light. The wooden floor is polished so that you click along clinically, or carpet so that you pad soundlessly, resting the feet while the eyes have at the wall' (15).

To pause for a moment, it is worth noticing that O'Doherty has introduced sound into his formulation of the gallery, yet he does not pick up that the sound is in excess of the art; the clicking heels or padding feet sounds are usually not part of the artwork. Instead, he bypasses this anomaly without further discussion and continues his portrayal of the modernist frame. Everything that is not art is removed from the rooms, leading to the concept that literally everything housed within the art gallery is in fact art (O'Doherty points out that the fire hose therefore becomes an 'esthetic conundrum'). These modernist spaces become the site for spiritual-like contemplation of art objects and the audience attends exhibitions in a hushed manner, speaking quietly, if they must at all. This is an isolated experience where the individual, even when accompanied by another person, experiences an individual artwork in isolation. Thus the modernist artwork, singular/timeless/utopian, is met by the individual outside of their daily life and free from distraction. However sequestered from the everyday the gallery becomes, it will forever be intruded upon by sound, a troubling source of distraction for any modernist art gallery.

When Paul Hegarty exclaims, 'Sound is totally banished from the gallery' (2007, 77), he does so with the full knowledge that this is never possible. While the white cube can be visually isolated, it is nearly impossible to completely isolate the space from the outside world, not least in relation to sounds from inside and outside of its bounds. Outside sounds, everyday sounds and noise in general enter the art gallery. For example:

- Sounds of traffic (cars, bikes, aircraft, sirens), birds and weather (storms, rain, wind and thunder)
- The sounds in surrounding spaces (footsteps from the rooms above the gallery)
- Sounds from the audience (conversation, footsteps, non-verbal sounds such as coughing and sneezing)
- The sounds from the museum building, bookshop and restaurant (air conditioning, cash registers, the coffee machine)
- The sounds produced by artworks in adjoining galleries

Much has been said, although considerably less has been written, about the problems of the white cube in terms of sound and its attendant issues with regard to isolating sound, dampening reverberation and keeping exterior sounds at bay. While the gallery can effectively be sealed off visually, there is currently no such option for sound. Steven Connor explains that sound art as a form desires 'to burst boundaries, to tear down the walls, to break out of the confined space of the gallery' (2011, 129). Unbounded, sound presents a freedom not attainable for visual objects, which are confined by lines of sight. Sound is able to leave the immediate vicinity of its making and spread throughout the gallery and into the surrounding spaces.

> Galleries are designed according to the angular, not to say perpendicular logic dispensed and required by the eye. … Rather than moving from source to destination like a letter or a missile, sound diffuses in all directions, like a gas. Unlike light,

> sound goes round corners. Sound work makes us aware of the continuing emphasis upon division and partition that continues to exist even in the most radically revisable or polymorphous gallery space, because sound spreads and leaks, like odour. (129)

Sound certainly is an uncontainable event that 'spreads and leaks', yet the idea that sound is like a gas or an odour does not stand up to scrutiny as, unlike odour which can remain long after its cause has been removed, sound does not stay put, hanging around and moving with airflow. Beyond the poetics of Connor's statement, sound undoubtedly leaks, but it does so not like a liquid or a scent. Rather, it is a wave that emerges from a cause or a sound event, that radiates out, bouncing off perpendicular surfaces and vibrating through gallery walls. Even when a sounding work is fully surrounded by walls, it is possible for it to escape from the vessel intended to contain it. Consequently, 'Sound art comes not only through the wall, but round the corner and through the floor. Perhaps the greatest allure of sound for artists more than ever convinced of their libertarian vocation somehow to go over the institutional wall, is that sound, like an odour or a giggle, escapes' (129).

As sound escapes the institutional confines, it does so with glee and derision towards those it encroaches upon. The sounds of artworks from one gallery enter other spaces filled with non-sounding artworks, disturbing the peace. The white cube, cleaned of everything bar the singular art object, is filled with something its interior design can never fully remove. The desired sound content of the nearby video art piece becomes intrusive noise in the neighbouring space. The very design of the visually focused exhibition room aids in this intrusion as its hard surfaces readily reflect sound, helping it spread from one place to another. A multitude of words could fill the pages of this book in describing various strategies for handling sounding works in the art museum and gallery: sound dampening, air-locking, containment within headphones, turning down the volume, mixing sound levels across multiple works and ignoring the audio intrusion altogether. This book, however, is not about the sound problems of the art gallery, nor is it about discussing strategies for the curation of soundful exhibitions. Rather *Gallery Sound* takes the gallery space as a generative architecture in which sound is a continual undercurrent and a place where artists have employed sound within its bounds and used the gallery as a productive space.

Gallery Sound is made up of three chapters, which are in turn divided into smaller sections. The first chapter, 'The Empty-sounding Gallery', takes as its point of departure the gallery as void, a space that has been stripped of objects and emptied of all physical art so as to leave a vacant, empty white space. While there have been numerous exhibitions of the void, these iterations of the gallery space are understood to be part of a trajectory of explicitly visual art practice that began with Yves Klein. Drawing on the image of the void, 'The Empty-sounding Gallery' focuses on a series of experiments that occurred in and around 1969, where artists and composers explored the empty gallery as a site for generating sonic and experientially focused practices.

The works under investigation engage, in the first instance, in (un)sounding the gallery space and, in the second, with filling the empty gallery with sound. For these works, the gallery was emptied of all objects, including art objects, and sound within the exhibition spaces was either substantially reduced by dampening the space with acoustic materials and thereby quietening it, or sound was radically increased through high-volume amplification through speakers. I wish to read these works as a critique of the modernist interior design of the art gallery, questioning the assumption that art was a purely visual exploit through practices that were explicitly sensory and experiential. By dampening the sound within the art space, Robert Irwin, James Turrell, Michael Asher and Bruce Nauman drew attention to the ubiquity of sound and its role in our experience not just of art but of the world. Nauman, La Monte Young and Alvin Lucier placed sounds into the empty space, playing audio into a highly reverberant container that reflected it off the hard flat gallery surfaces to create a reflection of previous events (in the case of Nauman) and sound-saturated architecture (in the case of Young and Lucier). Visually empty galleries (as they appear in the photographic documentation) in these cases are anything but empty in terms of the sonic environment.

The second chapter, 'Noises in the Gallery', explores sound that, although usually considered noise, has been exploited in recent arts practices. The noises I am hearing in these instances can be high in volume – the sonic rush of the aeroplane landing thrust over the gallery or the rush of loud audio emanating from an oversized sound system housed within the white cube. Noise also presents itself as little more than a murmur – the pinging of the cash register or the art world gossip shared over a glass of chardonnay at a star-studded exhibition opening.

Art museums have become very noisy places as art tourism and blockbuster installations have become a central element of the art institution. The Turbine Hall at the Tate Modern, for example, is far from a hushed space for the quiet contemplation of genius; rather, inflated art installations compete with both the gigantic scale of the hall and the massive audiences who attend the museum every year. Artists such as Olafur Eliasson and Bruce Nauman, who will be discussed in this chapter, have utilized this venue for heavy-hitting installations and audiences have flocked to the venue to experience the new vision of contemporary art.

Chapter 3 will examine the relationship (or exchanges) between musical performance and the art gallery. It is, of course, commonplace for the art gallery to host concerts, engaging musicians to perform background music. However, 'Musical Galleries' is not so much interested in musicians simply using the gallery as an alternative concert hall, rock venue or club, but rather it focuses on how the use of the gallery has transformed music and how the art space has itself been transformed by music.

Focusing again on 1969 and a series of performances by the minimalist composers Philip Glass and Steve Reich, I ask the question 'Why was the art institution interested in having music performed in its art spaces?' It will be shown that the desire for new experimental practices led an art audience to embrace music in a manner that was difficult for the institution of music to replicate.

Art galleries have on occasion literally shaped music, generating practices that are forced by the architecture of the exhibition space to change the performance of the music itself. Events such as those held at Off Site in Tokyo and impermanent.audio in Sydney were shaped by the fragile setting of the artist-run gallery – fragile in the sense of being housed in a residential area in the case of Off Site and fragile in the sense of a tiny budget in the case of impermanent.audio.

Finally, the use of music as the medium of a highly produced style of contemporary art installation will be the focus of the final section. Artists like Marco Fusinato, Ragnar Kjartansson, Angelica Mesiti, Ari Benjamin Meyers, Marina Rosenfeld and Anri Sala will be discussed predominantly for their employment of music as the medium of their practice, and for the use of audio amplification systems that are beyond the regular minimal amplification expected in the art gallery context.

Thus far I have not employed the term 'sound art' in more than a passing manner. I have stated my view of the term in numerous texts[6] and will address it here only briefly as I believe far too much ink has been spent trying to evaluate this term, ink often wasted in its defence. Put simply, if there is no such thing as silence then the term sound art is redundant. Dan Flavin's work, for example, produces a sound, but it is not sound art in the same way that we can say that, in spite of the fact that his works are made from fluorescent tubes, they are not 'fluorescent tube art'. To my mind, the category of sound art is as valid and interesting as the categories of marble art or oil paint art, or cut-offs-of-fabric-sewn-together-to-form-a-quilt art and so on. If the term sound art were needed, then we would also need to accept the term 'sound music' as a valid category! Nonetheless, no matter what I think of the term 'sound art', there is little point in railing against something that has become common currency. *Gallery Sound* is not a book about sound art; rather, it is a book that listens closely to the sounds that are found within the spaces intended for the exhibition of art, and it listens to the works of artists who have heard the environment of exhibition as being ripe for art and music-making.

Up front I need to state that *Gallery Sound* is not conceived of as a survey of sounding practices within the art gallery, nor am I concerned with who did what first. Rather the book follows ideas around gallery sound and illustrates these ideas with examples. It is hoped that the reader will know of numerous other examples and counter examples that are not included here. The reader made aware of the sounding environment of the art gallery will, it is anticipated, take this awareness with them on subsequent visits to the art gallery, thinking and listening as they do so. A warning: you might not like what you hear!

1

The empty-sounding gallery

The 1960s were an extremely productive time for the arts, and this is certainly the case for art and music. The vanguard of Western art and music shifted away from high modernism and into experimentalism, and in the process took on a range of experimental practices, practices that slid across old demarcations, moving fluidly between disciplinary boundaries. One aspect of this shift in the visual arts was that a number of artists, like those who will be discussed here, developed an awareness that audience members always perceived their own experiencing bodies while in the art gallery. Artists and musicians including Robert Irwin, James Turrell, Michael Asher, Bruce Nauman, La Monte Young and Alvin Lucier (all who form the case studies in this chapter) developed approaches to art-making that did not expect the audience to simply stand in front of an inert artwork in order to have an art experience delivered to them. Instead, audience members encountered a series of practices within the gallery context that were not only non-visual but were also non-representational: they did not represent things in the world but also they did not represent experiences, they *were* experiences. Sound played a pivotal role in the development of these experimental practices that engaged audiences on an experiential level, giving audiences in the late 1960s an experience within the gallery that was not expected at the time and one that was, for many, rather unknown.

'The Empty-sounding Gallery' will focus on six artists and composers who were all experimenting with the experiencing body of their audience and with sound. It will be demonstrated that 1969 was a watershed moment in this context, with all of these artists and composers making pivotal works in that year. There is little to tangibly connect these artists and composers at the time, although some of them may certainly have known each other and each other's work. The works explored in this chapter were not solely exhibited in New York and as such it is more than likely the artists would not have been aware of what one another was producing and exhibiting at this time. I also want to point out that this is not a period where sound suddenly became a new medium of art or music. For starters, sound had always been an element of music. In terms of art, as already argued, sound has always been in the art gallery and inextricably linked to artworks. Sound as a medium within art had also been around for some time, having become prevalent in the 1960s through the experiments of Fluxus, in Happenings, and in the burgeoning practices of installation, performance and conceptual art, all of which were filled with sound.

Rather than try to understand sound within the practices discussed below as being somehow new or as indicative of a turn from the visual to the aural, I would say there is a shift from the artwork as a stand-alone singular object (one that exists in time and space) to art that is received by an experiencing audience who, by bringing their bodies and their minds along for the art experience, cannot help but engage their various senses as they encounter these works. We cannot, after all, leave our bodies behind as we walk around the art gallery. As well as engaging the senses of the audience, the works examined in this section are housed within what I am naming 'the empty-sounding gallery'. In using this term, I am referring to galleries that are pared back to bare white walls in the modernist style of the white cube, and in which identifiable art objects have all but vanished. The galleries sound empty – they are highly reflective rooms where sound bounces around them in a manner that emphasizes their emptiness. The galleries also 'sound' the exhibition environment in the sense that the empty interior architecture creates the sounding arts practices that will be under discussion. The galleries in question here are empty, almost becoming a void, and it is within this voided space that sound becomes generative, no longer an annoyance to be tolerated. The almost complete lack of visual interest is a strategy employed so as to shift the visitor's attention away from viewing and onto hearing, sensing and experiencing.

a Silence and the void

Brian O'Doherty begins his article 'The Gallery as a Gesture' by stating that a new type of art space with new imperatives began to appear between the 1920s and 1970s, a gallery space that was itself as distinct as the art shown within it: 'The new god, extensive, homogeneous space, flowed easily into every part of the gallery. All impediments except "art" were removed.' He goes on to ask, 'Is the empty gallery ... modernism's greatest invention?' (O'Doherty 1999, 87).

In O'Doherty's reading of the white cube, the space itself actually becomes the artwork and the rhetoric of the modernist gallery, stripped of all elements that are in excess of the artwork, is taken a step further. Rather than straightforwardly emptying the room of anything other than the individual, contained art object (like ornamentation, everyday objects, natural light, coloured walls, outside sound and so on), in the examples discussed below anything resembling an art object has also been removed. Now we have the greatest invention of them all, the white cube decluttered of everything except itself.

Certainly the most well-known exhibition of empty space is Yves Klein's The Void, shown at Galerie Iris Clert in Paris in the spring of 1958. For the exhibition Klein removed all the objects from the gallery and painted the walls white. At the opening the patrons drank Yves Klein blue cocktails after being admitted by two Republican guards to what for all intents and purposes was an empty space or, perhaps, a gallery framing the 'immaterial', a 'pictorial sensibility invisible to the naked eye' (Copeland 2009). Klein also presented an empty white room, entitled *Salle du Vide* (Void Room), in the Museum Haus Lange in Krefeld, Germany (1961).

Following on from Klein's void, a number of related exhibitions occurred, which O'Doherty regards as examples of what he termed the 'gallery gesture'. Perhaps the most consistent of these gestures occur in the work of the artists associated with 'institutional critique'. Here the institution of art, including its exhibition spaces, were the subject of systemic critique, of which Daniel Buren's first solo exhibition, *Il s'agit de voir* (On Seeing), held in October 1968, is a prime example. Buren sealed off the Galleria Apollinaire in Milan for the full duration of the exhibition, turning the empty gallery into an excluded space. The audience is not allowed to enter and consequently can only imagine what is being kept from them, although what is being withheld is, of course, actually the experience of entering the gallery – whether there are objects to contemplate or not is beside the point. Other examples include Robert Barry's touring exhibition of 1969–70 entitled Closed Gallery Piece. This exhibition was just that, a closed gallery. Similarly, Robert Irwin's Experimental Situation (Ace Gallery, Los Angeles 1970) was also an empty gallery, while Michael Asher's empty galleries were modified, for example walls were removed (Clare Copley Gallery 1974) or sanded down to the extent that the internal wall structure under the clean white paint was exposed (Franco Toselli Gallery 1973). Laurie Parsons, meanwhile, presented an empty gallery for an exhibition in 1990; in this instance, not only was the gallery space empty, but the invitation to the exhibition included neither the title of the show nor the name of the artist. The empty gallery was also the subject and content of a major exhibition at the Pompidou in Paris entitled Voids, A Retrospective (2009), for which a total of nine empty gallery works by nine artists were exhibited.

By displaying the gallery itself as art, we are led to think about its role in the art institution and the types of elements and practices within the culture of exhibition that we take for granted. These voided exhibition spaces are, of course, not voids, just as silence is not silence; on the contrary, they still contain air and as such they contain sounds and scents. The audience walking through these empty spaces brings noises with them – for example, the sound of footsteps or the rattle of a cleared throat. The outside manages to find a way into all of these spaces; the sounds emanating from nearby galleries and noisy corridors enter, as do everyday traffic noises and hostile weather sounds. The void, we find, is neither silent nor empty.

b Silence

The void, found in space for example, is truly silent as sound waves cannot travel through it and the expectation of an empty gallery might be that it too is quiet, silent even. Metaphorically speaking, the gallery that is void of content is quiet in its lack of art, yet an empty gallery is in actuality an acoustically noisy space because it is completely bare, resulting in a room that becomes wildly reverberant and echoic. We have probably experienced this feeling in an unoccupied house, one that does not have furniture or carpet. In these domestic spaces, footsteps and voices are seemingly amplified by the hard surfaces that surround us. In the gallery, sound bounces off the walls and, without artworks to break up the flat surfaces, sounds made within the space are intensified. For many, the art museum is a quiet space, created for the hushed contemplation of masterpieces, so when we enter the gallery we quieten our voices and tread lightly. Yet we would be hard pressed to think of the enclosed architecture of a gallery space as being anything like silent. Perhaps it is the case that we lower our voices out of respect for the significance of the art in front of us; if so, this silence has significance in this section of *Gallery Sound* because it is unattainable, and quite likely impossible. Any discussion of silence within the context of the arts must include John Cage and in particular two instances of 'silence'. These stories have been recounted many times and so I will describe them swiftly before unpacking their value for this particular discussion.

4′33″ (1952) is certainly John Cage's most influential and well-known composition. The piece comprised three movements that together amount to the duration of four minutes and thirty-three seconds, all of which are performed following the musical instruction *tacet*, indicating that a voice or instrument is silent. In its inaugural performance on 29 August 1952, the pianist David Tudor sat in front of a piano without depressing a single key over the course of the recital; instead, he lowered and raised the keyboard cover to signal the beginning and end of each of the three movements that comprise the piece. While the musician is instructed not to perform any sound on their instrument, the piece itself is anything but silent. With the instrumental sound content removed from the performance, all the other sounds that are present within the concert hall are brought to the fore. Rustling, coughing, creaking floorboards, whispers, as well as environmental sounds such as rain, cars and aeroplanes overhead are heard loud and clear. Put simply there is no silence in *4′33″* and the composition makes abundantly clear that true silence is impossible.

4′33″ was influenced by an earlier experience that has a similar trajectory in that an imagined silence allows noise to be brought to the fore. Cage had been interested in 'all sound' and as a result sought out very loud sounds and very quiet sounds. This search led him to the anechoic chamber, a room engineered to prevent any sounds present in the space from reflecting off the chamber's surfaces. Anechoic chambers reduce the reflection of sound within an enclosed space, thanks to their acoustically treated walls. The walls themselves look like lavish fetish decoration, all spiky and padded. The design of the room is such that sounds produced within the space produce little to no reverberation or echo (an effect referred to as dampening), while at the same time preventing extraneous sound entering from outside. The technology is designed for experimental purposes, specifically to isolate where a sound emanates from in mechanical equipment such as engines or even fighter jets. A somewhat unexpected consequence of the design of this technology is that it also isolates any person who enters it, removing them from their normal auditory environment. We locate ourselves in space based partly on what we hear around us, including the sound reflected off walls, which gives us an indication of the volume of the space we find ourselves in because of the reverberation within. The anechoic chamber has the effect of creating a void-like experience. If the lights are turned off, the room is extremely dark, causing subjects to lose their sense of relationship to the space they are in. As much as this space might then be expected to allow the subject entering into it to experience a true silence, however, an unexpected ancillary effect of being in this space is that one becomes aware of the sounds of one's own body as never before, sounds both familiar (such as the heartbeat) and unknown (such as the sounds of one's nervous system). Cage visited Harvard University's anechoic chamber in 1951 and, to his surprise, while inside he found that the room was not silent at all; he could still hear sounds. This in itself is an interesting insight and one that is actuated when one experiences an anechoic chamber. The space is only silent as long as nothing inside makes a sound, no matter how slight that sound might be, because in this space sounds that would normally be lost in the ambient sounds of the everyday environment are intensified through extreme isolation.

The story goes that Cage heard a high and a low sound while inside the anechoic chamber, and was told by the room's engineer when he exited the room and asked what these sounds were that 'the high one was your nervous system in operation. The low one was your blood in circulation' (Cage 1967, 134). Cage, at the time of his visit, was in the process of extending the range of what sounds could count as musical to encompass all sounds, and the chamber in effect allowed him to extend his range of possible sounds further by including sounds created inside the body that are usually inaudible to both the sound maker and anyone who is standing nearby. This is of interest to Douglas Kahn in large part because the anecdote of Cage's visit to the anechoic chamber (recounted repeatedly by the composer) includes a nod to 'all sounds' yet at the same time also seems to go against his belief in 'letting sounds be themselves'. For Kahn, this can be explained by understanding that the tale meant that Cage 'was able to listen and at the same time allow discursiveness to intrude in the experience' (1999, 190). That is, the story requires a scientific description to do its job – Cage needs to tell us what the sounds are so we know it was not some type of strange hallucination that only Cage himself could experience. More interesting than the actuality of the sounds (and the details of the explanation have since been questioned) is the fact that even in the most silent of environments there is still sound to be attended to.

My own experience of an anechoic chamber occurred at the Technische Universität Berlin. The chamber housed at the university is 50 square metres in floor space. While a visiting professor at the university in 2015, I took a group of students into the chamber where the technician was more than pleased to turn off the lights and close us in for a short period of time. Once inside the quiet space we sat with the lights turned off. The room was so dark you could not see your hand in front of your face, so dark that it made no difference to what you could see if your eyes were open or closed. In terms of what I heard, at the time of entering the room I had the remains of a mild head cold, and as a result I was experiencing sinus pressure and some tinnitus, the sound of which was dramatically heightened in the chamber. I felt radically isolated. By this I mean I felt totally isolated from my surrounds but very close to my internal body sounds and especially my breath. There is total isolation in the darkness, but this is accompanied by an extreme intimacy with the sound of your body. These sounds, indeed, are so present that it is resolutely not possible to say that one experiences silence in the anechoic chamber acoustically.

Many of the artists associated with the Light and Space movement are linked to this piece of experimental technology. Art historian

Dawna Schuld points to Robert Irwin and James Turrell (who will be discussed below) as well as Doug Wheeler, Maria Nordman and Eric Orr, all of whom spent time in anechoic chambers 'experimenting with experience' (Schuld 2011, 111). Why were artists drawn to the chamber designed to control the acoustic conditions of a room? One possible explanation is that the chamber, through its silencing of space, severely reduces the auditory stimuli presented to subjects within. While on the face of it a lack of stimulation could be considered the very opposite of what is expected of the experience of art, as will be shown below, people – whether composers, artists or individuals entering the chamber – have very similar experiences induced by the extreme lack of auditory and visual stimulation. Thus it can be suggested that Cage's experience was no different from that of many others and, in the hands of Turrell and Irwin, this very fact – that is, the commonality of the experience – made it possible to conceptualize and plan for an artwork that would use these physiological and psychological experiences as its content.

c Sense of sensing: Robert Irwin and James Turrell

Michael Auping, in a chapter entitled 'Stealth Architecture' (a term with boundless possibilities), puts it succinctly: 'One empty room is not always the same as another' (2011, 88). The Southern Californian Light and Space artists pare back their art to the brink of non-existence, a mere glimmer of light or an installed window tint. If we can accept light as a logical basis for art, then, following the same line of argument, we must accept sound as a possible content or medium of art. During the 1960s and into the 1970s, a strand of art thinking developed in which the object-hood of the artwork, its singularity and thingness, was replaced by the environment, signalling a shift 'from a thing being framed by a room to the room being the thing' (80).

This approach ties very neatly into the core arguments posited in this book, namely that the context for the exhibition of sounding artworks – the gallery – is not only a framing device but also a crucial component of those works, one that creates content and meaning. Therefore, examining these works focuses not on a given media or medium but, rather, on practices that are founded on the perceptions of the audience and the psychological outcomes that are created through an extremely minimal (in terms of means) approach to art-making. The Light and Space artists critically experimented with perception as the sum total of their work. At the core of these experiments is an approach that deprives the senses of certain stimuli and, conversely, produces a powerful effect in the minds of the audience. The radical stripping back of sound sensation occurred in the experiments undertaken in the late 1960s by Irwin and Turrell as part of the Art and Technology project instigated by the Los Angeles County Museum of Art. The results of their investigations were surprising in that they found that an overall reduction of sensory input conversely produced intensified sensory experiences.

Sensory deprivation would seem to be a logical reference point when thinking about these kinds of empty gallery practices. When audiences are confronted with galleries devoid of the visual art object and any specific point of visual focus, we might imagine that we are dealing with an art practice intent on engendering sensory deprivation, specifically a visual deprivation. How is an individual to deal with the lack of an object for them to find a (sensory) point of focus or to, quite literally, *see* something of interest? There is one key assumption in play here, which is based on our general understanding of visual art. We go to an art gallery to see something and as such we expect to have a visual experience. If we are used to visiting contemporary art spaces, then we might expect our visual experience to occur alongside other sensory experiences, such as sound, smell, taste and touch. Remove the visual altogether and the audience must instantly adjust their expectations. Remove all sensory content and the audience, as a whole, may well be at a loss as to how they are expected to have an art experience at all.

Numerous artists have explicitly explored sense deprivation by placing themselves in extreme situations. An example from the early work of Australian artist Stelarc is *Event for Support Structure* (1979), for which he spent seventy-five hours wedged between two planks of wood with his eyes and mouth stitched together. American artist Chris Burden performed a series of works in which he was held in place for extended durations, as well as works that called for long periods of doing very little within the confines of the art gallery. For example, *Five Day Locker Piece* (1971) required Burden to spend five days inside a locker, while for *Doomed* (1975) the artist spent forty-five hours under a plate of glass in the Museum of Contemporary Art, Chicago. Marina Abramović has on numerous occasions put herself in situations of sustained endurance with exceedingly low amounts of sensory interest. Perhaps the most extreme version of these works was *The Artist is Present*, for which she sat stationary in a chair in front of audience members for eight hours a day from 14 March to 31 May 2010. The long duration of the piece meant that the artist had very little in the way of sensory stimulus, or little in the way of changing stimulus as she sat in the same gallery day in and day out. While these artists were deprived of their everyday lives and the daily actions that occurred within, it could certainly be argued that the work was not truly sensory deprivation. That is, there is a marked reduction in stimuli, but the artists' bodies are still actively receiving stimulation in that they feel the discomfort of being in confined spaces or fixed poses, or are faced with the experience of the audience members in the case of Abramović. As Schuld explains, there is a difference between 'sensory deprivation' and the extreme reduction of sensory stimuli as the subjects are not literally deprived of their senses, which of course remained intact and functioning (2010, 223).

The empty-sounding gallery asks far less from its audience than the performance artists mentioned above asked of themselves. Rather than putting the audience in extreme situations, the artists here create environments within the gallery space that are devoid of singular objects. Specific, tangible architectural elements are smoothed out, not to flatten the space but, rather, to make its edges and corners indistinct. Here we have a slippage between the artist being at the centre – the artist as feeling/sensing maker – and the audience as feeling/sensing receptor. We can think about this in relation to art objects and also in terms of minimal art of the 1960s and early 1970s. Faced by extremely minimal artworks the audience questions what is expected of them. Given the lack of visual content, how are they supposed to act in front of these works? Two artists, Robert Irwin and James Turrell, specifically worked with the sensory deprivation afforded by access to an anechoic chamber for an extended period of time. They discovered that, 'Sitting in these reduced surroundings (the anechoic chamber) was exhausting; rather than depriving the subject of the senses of sight and hearing, the lack of focal markers proved to heighten them, causing the subject to strain his eyes and ears, searching for something upon which to focus his attention' (221).

In 1966 Maurice Tuchman initiated the Art and Technology Program while he was a curator at the Los Angeles County Museum of Art.[1] He planned to pair up a range of artists with large Californian corporations, such as Ampex, General Electrics, Hudson Institute, Jet Propulsion Laboratory, Litton Industries and the Rand Corporation (to name a few). The corporations predominantly worked across engineering and scientific interests, often directed towards aeronautic and military ends. Tuchman signed up these technologically focused corporations with some of the best-known artists working at the time, including Andy Warhol, Richard Serra, Robert Rauschenberg, Tony Smith and Roy Lichtenstein. Robert Irwin was approached early in the project and subsequently went on a number of tours of research facilities. As Tuchman writes, however, 'It was evident even during this preliminary view of a corporation that Irwin ... was not interested so much in industrial fabricating techniques as in the more abstract areas of theoretical experiments in perceptual psychology' (1971, 127).

In 1969, Irwin teamed up with James Turrell to work with the Garrett Corporation, working closely with Dr Ed Wortz, head of the life sciences department. Part of the original project conceived by these three was a sensory deprivation space within a gallery. A single person would be allowed into the gallery that was created from anechoic chamber technology. The gallery would be totally dark and sound dampened and the individual audience member would then remain in the space for a duration of between six and fifteen minutes (130). While this period of exposure to the chamber might seem short, for the uninitiated this duration could have been exceedingly confronting. Irwin had initially toured Lockheed Aircraft Corporation's Rye Canyon Research Center where there was an anechoic chamber that was used to test human responses to sensory phenomena. After coming across the chamber Irwin wanted to use one for experimental purposes. He ended up using a chamber at UCLA that he described as being 'a particularly fine one; it was suspended so that even the sound of the rotation of the earth was not reflected in it, or any sounds being bounced through the earth' (Weschler and Irwin 1982, 128).

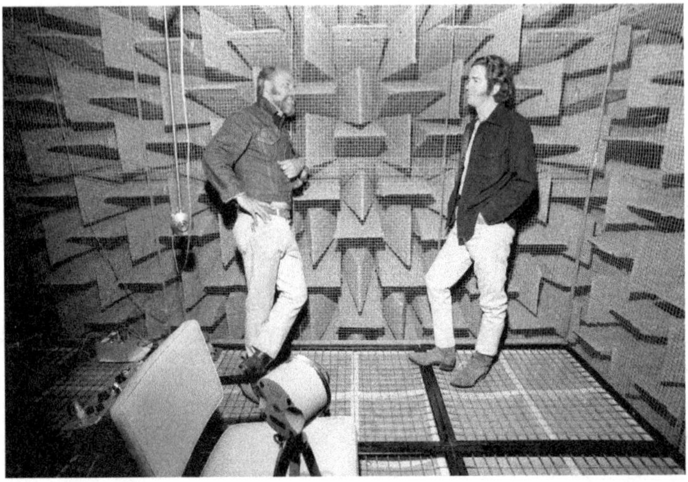

FIGURE 4 Robert Irwin and James Turrell inside the anechoic chamber at UCLA, 1969. ©Malcolm Lubliner Photography.

Irwin describes how the two artists would enter the chamber in which neither light nor sound could enter once it was closed. Left only with the sounds they themselves created, they would sit in there for extended stretches of time – by Irwin's account as long as eight hours (128). These considerable durations tested the artists' perceptual ability and also noticeably shifted their awareness of how they sensed the world. Irwin describes how these periods in the chamber effected his sensory experience writing: 'After I'd sat in there for six hours, for instance, and then got up and walked back home down the same street I'd come in on, the trees were still trees, and the street was still a street, and the houses were still houses, but the world did not look the same; it was very, very noticeably altered' (128). This altering of perceptual understanding is key to many of the works being discussed in this chapter. The audience is not simply attending an installation to receive a passive visual experience; instead, they are experiencing a work that could actually alter their perceptual awareness. This was to be a very exciting impetus to art-making for Irwin and Turrell and it drove them to experiment with the chamber, using it as a means not only to investigate their own experience and perception, but also to experiment with other subjects who participated in their projects.

The experiences of a group of subjects were systematically surveyed as part of the development of the project. Schuld explains the reaction of the subjects in the following way: 'Doing nothing was extremely disconcerting to subjects new to the project and they would report feeling uncomfortable after brief periods (fewer than ten minutes) while the artists would happily spend hours in the chamber' (2010, 230). The subjects who were placed within the chamber and later asked about their experiences had similar responses to those of the artists. Given the similarities of experience, it was clear to Irwin and Turrell that these lived experiences could become the stuff of the exhibition, rather than a tangible or physical art object. Irwin and Turrell planned to bring scientific, neuro-psychological and cognitive science knowledges to a wider audience through the use of technology within the gallery: 'In this environment, where science and art occupied mutually non-transgressible realms, Robert Irwin and James Turrell adopted a middle position. Coincident with cognitive psychology, they asserted that felt experience is the essential *matter* of art rather than the stuff of traditional artistic media' (234).

Schuld places the work of the Californian artists in the context of scientific and technological developments as well as shifts in cognitive psychology. For her, this was a situation that was vastly different from that of the East Coast artists who at the time were involved in a discussion of the limits of minimalism and the function of the white cube. The situational understanding of an art based on experience goes further than the theatrical critique of an audience exploring the relationship between themselves and an object in front of them. While in the end no tangible exhibition came from the collaboration between the three (with Turrell walking away from the project before it reached completion), the understanding of the senses that the project brought to Irwin and Turrell would follow them throughout their subsequent careers.

d Unified sensory situation: Michael Asher

Michael Asher has consistently drawn attention to the role of the gallery within the mechanisms of art (the art institution: its systems of display, its commercial value systems and the institutional systems of the art museum). More often than not, Asher's exhibitions are void of any singular art object; instead, the object of his artwork is the gallery itself. Towards this end he has removed gallery walls and entranceways, sanded walls, created walls from air-conditioning units and swapped galleries between locations. All of these examples fit within a history of the empty gallery within visual art, but two early works in particular are crucial for thinking about sound and silence within an empty gallery and the sensory experience of the audience.

In November 1969 Asher installed a room within the La Jolla Museum of Art in San Diego, California. While there are very few photographs taken of the untitled installation, one that has often been reproduced as a document of the exhibition is telling (see Figure 3, page 13). The dark image illustrates a blank space with fluorescent light (that has been over exposed and creates a flare) and from which it is extremely hard to discern what the installation consisted of. While there is very little photographic documentation, it is critical to understanding the installation that attention be paid to its sensory elements; what did it feel like to experience this work? While the photographic documentation gives little in the way of clues to answer this question, Asher has described the installation in detail (Asher was extremely thorough in his technical description of these installations) and there are also a small number of reviews from the time. He states of the work: 'The materials and the structure prevented the work from being perceived in exclusively visual and objectified terms. The constructed space functioned as a container for perceptual phenomena leading beyond the usual wall and floor references in the placement of works of art in a gallery' (Asher 1983, 20).

The gallery was painted white and the lighting was designed to be 'diffused from the centre of the room toward the periphery' (Peltomäki 2010, 22). The walls were especially built for the exhibition, indicative of Asher's attention to detail, which was initiated in this exhibition and would come to be common in his later work. Thus far we can discern these elements of the installation from the photograph, but there is another layer to this seemingly empty gallery. Asher carpeted the floor in thick white shagpile. The original ceiling already had sound-dampening material installed; thus the combination of floor and ceiling dampening quietened the space and made for a noticeably different acoustic from the other galleries within the museum. The gallery walls were not acoustically treated, allowing sound to be reflected horizontally.

Into this environment Asher played a sine tone generated by an oscillator, amplifier and a speaker placed behind a wall. The tone was set to a low eighty-five hertz, creating a continuous deep sound that would have been constantly present for the audience in spite of the fact that it was played at the very threshold of audibility. Asher described the effect as follows:

> The vertical surfaces responded to the sound frequency, which caused them to resonate as if they were tuned, while the horizontal surfaces, due to their sound-dampening effect, reduced the frequency. The cancellation of the sound waves occurred when these frequencies coincided. The sound waves cancelled each other out at a point exactly in the centre of the gallery and, on a diagonal axis, on the right hand side of each corner. Up to each point of sound wave cancellation, the sound increased gradually in intensity; whereas at the exact cancellation point none of the generated sound was heard. (1983, 18)

The effect of both the light diffusing from the centre of the space and the sound shifting in amplitude as the audience moved around the space created an immersive environment that responded to the individual's own movements. As Asher describes this: 'As with light, the use of sound had the capacity to confront the viewer's understanding of space as static, tactile, and formally structured (a dominant trend in art during this period in Southern California), with the notion of its temporality and dynamics' (20). A space that is seemingly empty is actually dynamic and changing in relation to a moving body. The viewer cannot help but engage in these dynamics as their physical movement changes their experience of the installation.

A second work, also untitled and from the same year, is even emptier than the La Jolla installation in that it relies solely on the interior architecture of the gallery. The work was built for the group show Spaces at the Museum of Modern Art, curated by Jennifer Licht, which ran from December 1969 to March 1970. The show included five discrete galleries that were occupied by Robert Morris, Dan Flavin, Larry Bell, F. E. Walther and Michael Asher. For the installation Asher had the walls that ran along the adjoining corridor constructed so that they would jut into the corridor's space, leaving two entry points for the visitors. Inside the gallery he lowered the ceiling to a height of 2.4 metres (from the original 4.26 metres). He constructed the room with walls filled with fibreglass sound insulation to heavily dampen the reverberation of the gallery space. In addition to this, the walls themselves were constructed on rubber wedges so that they were isolated from any vibration coming from within the building itself. Two layers of textured acoustical panelling were also installed on the floor and ceiling. The key difference between the installation for the La Jolla Museum and the one in Spaces was thus that the latter 'absorbed sound, as opposed to the previous work at the La Jolla Museum which reflected it' (24). This close attention to sound treatment is extremely rare within the gallery context and marks a clear interest in the sonic sensory experience intended for the audience. Asher also describes the aural experience of the work in close detail:

> Ambient sound from the exterior, such as street traffic, the interior, such as movement and voices of people in the corridor of the museum, as well as mechanical noises, such as the air delivery-and-return system of the Garden Wing, all merged and condensed on a diagonal axis at the two entry/exit openings. Because of the increased absorption on the entry/exit axis, the sound reached its lowest level toward the center of the installation. On the opposite diagonal axis sound steadily decreased, gradually approaching complete absorption where the walls met in the corners of the installation. (24)

In addition to this, the space itself was unlit, the only light entering into the space shining in from the open entranceways. Where the room was at its darkest was also where sound was most absorbed, creating a very quiet and dark environment. This was a radically empty space; empty of art objects, of light and of sound.

Like the subject in an anechoic chamber, audiences within an art environment that lacks a point of visual focus tend to focus on their sensorial and phenomenological engagement with the space they find themselves in. They might feel the carpet on their toes (audience members were asked to remove their shoes for the exhibition at La Jolla) or watch the shape of their own shadow as they moved around the room. Thomas H. Garver, who reviewed the exhibition at La Jolla for *Artforum*, suggests something similar, but adds that the experience turned out to be too much for some. He writes: 'The sensory effect of the room was both quiescent and intense. As the room neither "showed" anything nor "did" anything, some spectators suffered an immediate esthetic collapse and left at once' (Garver 1970, 75).

For Garver, the lack of sensory input actually creates an intensification of sensory experiences, heightening the audiences' awareness of their visual, aural and tactile response to the installation. He also points to a theatricality of the work that, due to it 'doing' very little, elicits a solo performance from the audience member inside the work before them. In discussing the Spaces exhibition, meanwhile, art critic Carter Ratcliff points to the fact that audience members must physically enter the artwork. For him this is fundamentally different from standing in front of a painting or even walking around a sculptural object: 'Participation is automatic, denied to no one' (Ratcliff 1970, 78). However, Ratcliff was highly critical of the exhibition, declaring that he had received more valuable experiences by riding in an elevator!

Asher's piece requires of its audience a re-evaluation of what presence is in terms of an exhibition. The audience are in the presence of an installation, but rather than the installation consisting of objects being installed in the gallery, the whole gallery here, emptied of other objects, becomes the installation. Berlin-based critic and artist Brandon LaBelle usefully describes this as creating 'opportunities for rethinking materiality in general by introducing the perceptual question of whether acoustical additions and subtractions may in the end come to constitute, quite literally, an artistic object or not' (LaBelle 2006, 89). In her paper on these two works, Kirsi Peltomäki, an academic whose core research interest is Michael Asher, argues that while there are no discrete art objects within the galleries, instead 'there was a comprehensive, multi-sensory space for museum visitors to enter' (Peltomäki 2014, 55). The audience has a deeply sensory experience in these two exhibitions precisely because the situation created by Asher draws attention to visual and aural experiences (or lack thereof) and to the sensing body.

Italian curator Germano Celant begins his article 'Artspaces', written in 1975, by demarcating exhibition practices that simply use the gallery 'as a "bed"' from those that 'take the space in its *entirety*' [italics in original] (1975, 116). In the article he traces a history of artistic use of space through a series of categories that ends with 'Experience Space'. These spaces, according to Celant, '"test" one's own dimension and energy on a human scale' (116). With their physical and spatial boundaries reduced through optical and auditory design, 'Each space, according to the degree of reduction or expansion of simple phenomena, purposely allows a "descent into the self"' (116). Accordingly, the lack of stimulation and dampening of sensory input causes audience members to concentrate on themselves and on their own experience of the space, heightening awareness of their senses. Celant ends in poetic fashion describing the audience members' descent into the self as drawing out the need to be alone with one's experience of the space, calm and alert to it: 'In a field empty of reference points, the person's attention turns towards himself, as in Nauman's corridors and tactile walls' (116).

For Asher, 'Sound had the capacity to confront the viewer's understanding of space as static, tactile, and formally structured' (1983, 20). Thus the empty gallery that has been subtly transformed to dampen the sound reflection within can draw its audiences' attention to the space and the manner in which they come to know it through their senses. As with Asher's empty galleries, Bruce Nauman produced the empty-sounding gallery through material structures placed within the gallery that served to dampen sound while activating an awareness of the sensing body in his audience.

e Rendered acoustical: Bruce Nauman

Bruce Nauman's utilization of sound as a medium can be found throughout his extensive career but in its most concentrated form in the late 1960s and early 1970s. There is a diverse range of approaches to the use of sound within his works, such as recording a scream and placing it in a 240-kg block of concrete (*Concrete Tape Recorder Piece* (1968)), producing sounds made by three performers falling back onto a gallery wall (*Performance Arena* (1969)), playing a violin tuned to the notes D, E, A and D (*Violin Tuned D.E.A.D* (1969)), stamping in his studio (*Stamping in the Studio* (1968)), and playing a tape recording of himself reciting anagrams of the phrase 'lighted steel channel' (*Steel Channel Piece* (1968)). All of the works that actively engage sound can be understood within the wider themes of the artist's overall practice as Nauman never uses sound as a stand-alone medium. In recent years there have been some attempts to claim the use of sound in his works as a defining factor, but these attempts have been thwarted by the artist's complex approach to materials and media, much like attempts to label him a video artist, installation or post-minimalist artist.

Bruce Nauman made a lot of art in the mid-to-late 1960s – an understatement if ever there was one. Between 1965 and 1970 he created some one hundred and seventy catalogued works.[2] The majority of these were produced while living in California after finishing a graduate degree at the University of California, Davis. There the artist swiftly developed an international career in the new wave of post-minimalist sculpture. During this period, he instigated a trans-media approach to art-making, an approach that is at the centre of much contemporary art of our current period. Many of the works conceived of at this time are foundational and core to Nauman's oeuvre, and are repeatedly discussed in the literature, including his studio performances (recorded on film and video) and corridor works. At the centre of the works produced in the late 1960s is an exploration of the experiencing body of the audience. Marcia Tucker, in an early article on Nauman, states, 'To encounter one of these pieces is to experience basic phenomena that have been isolated, inverted, taken out of context, or progressively destroyed' (Tucker 1970, 38). Tucker points to phenomena being a medium of the work rather than something that is simply represented. Like the work of Asher, Irwin and Turrell, the experiences of the embodied spectator are not merely an effect of the material installation – instead, experience is the content of the piece. Nauman's ambivalence to the physical piece (its material presence) can be witnessed in a letter written in 1970 to his German art dealer Konrad Fischer.[3] The letter directs Fischer on the sale of the installation *Diagonal Sound Wall (Acoustic Wall)* (1970), which included a large acoustically treated wall. As Nauman explained, the sale of this piece included the plans for the construction of the work but may or may not comprise any of the materials that were used in the original exhibition. Similarly, as we will see below, Nauman's ambivalence is also evident in the fact that the instructions for the central wall were simply contracted out for fabrication, rather than needing to be the product of the artist's own labour.

In discussing Nauman's work from 1969 to 1974, Janet Kraynak describes 'a series of hybrid sculptural installations that assertively engage and act upon the beholder's body, senses, and mind' (Kraynak 2003, 23). She further elucidates: 'In some, empty space is rendered acoustical through recorded sounds of the artist yelling, laughing, exhaling; or through walls lined with thick acoustical materials that invite the viewer to touch and produce sound' (23). Originally these walls were constructed by Nauman from cheap wood and formed into tight physical corridors that were placed within an art gallery. Installations such as *Performance Corridor* (1969), *Green Light Corridor* (1970) and *Changing Light Corridor with Rooms* (1971) allowed the audience to experience the work without giving them things and objects to manipulate. In fact, for the artist it was important that he 'not allow ... people to make their own performance out of my art' (Sharp 2003b). In order to experience these works, audience members needed to enter into the highly restricted space of the corridor. From within this tight setting there is very little an audience member can do, other than slide himself or herself through it. As Nauman himself puts it, 'In the museum situations, [*Performance Corridor*] serves to severely restrict and then re-enforce the available audio, visual and kinaesthetic responses of anyone who walks in or around the wall' (Kraynak 2014, 113).

The installation *Diagonal Sound Wall (Acoustic Wall)* (1970) title might suggest that this work makes sound, yet it produces no sound at all; rather it dampens the acoustics, namely the sound reflection, within the gallery.[4] The work is formed from a wall, handmade out of acoustic materials that, as a result, means that it looks more like a mattress than anything else. The wall is installed diagonally in the gallery space at Konrad Fischer Galerie, slicing the small gallery in half, boxing in the front desk. In the corner of the gallery the wall leaves only a tight 50-cm gap for exhibition visitors to move from one side of the construction to the other. The diagonal installation allows for very tight corners, a physical structure that Nauman used in some of his other corridor installations, but in this work it also serves to produce an acoustic dead spot in the corner of the gallery.[5]

Nauman, in his letter to Konrad Fischer, explains the desired results of the installation: 'It not only changes sound, but you must pay attention to the pressure changes in your ears as you move

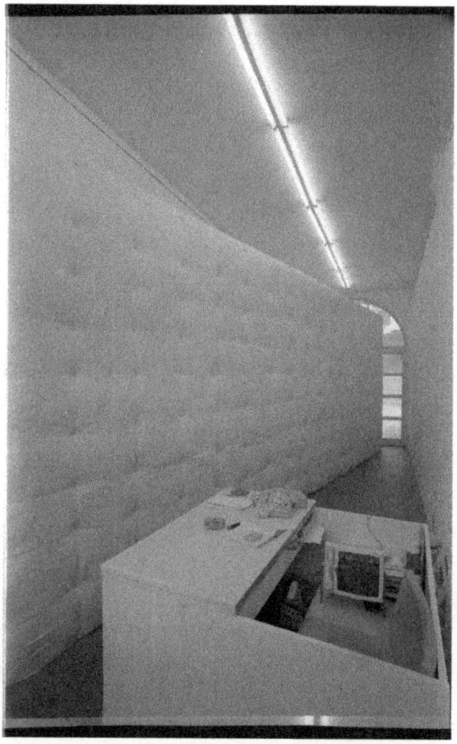

FIGURE 5 Bruce Nauman, *Diagonal Sound Wall (Acoustic Wall)* (1970). Courtesy of the Dorothee and Konrad Fischer Archive, Kunstsammlung Nordrhein-Westfalen, Düsseldorf.

near and away from the wall. ... It is a rather subtle effect until you have been in the area a few minutes.' Visitors experience *Diagonal Sound Wall* by moving through the gallery space, which is completely dominated by the padded wall. Gallery patrons would have walked into the space, squeezed past the desk and down to the tight end of the wall. They could then slip over to the other side that was completely empty and experience the tightening wedge on the opposite side. It is key to the experience of the work that the audience moves around the wall object and, as Nauman states, takes the time to notice the change in air pressure caused by the dampened sound space of the gallery.

Another piece from the same time is much tighter than *Diagonal Sound Wall* in form and has also been described as having a pressure effect on the ear of the audience members. For this work, *Acoustic Wedge (Sound Wedge – Double Wedge)* (1969–70), four walls connected to a single apex/point were built so as to create a series of wedge-shaped corridors. The audience is invited to enter the corridors and then to inch their way as far as they could towards the end point. Once wedged into the tight space, the acoustics would have transformed the sound within to make a quiet and dampened space. Willoughby Sharp interviewed Nauman extensively in two in-depth interviews, and in the second the artist described the effect that the combination of the corridor and soundproofing material created in relation to *Corridor Installation with Mirror – San Jose Installation* (1970–4). Nauman explains, 'The wall relied on soundproofing material which altered the sound of the corridor and also caused pressure on your ears' (Sharp 2003a, 134). Sharp follows this by stating, 'So space is *felt* with one's ears?' to which Nauman replies, 'Yeah that's right' (134). This feeling of pressure is critical to understanding the effect on the room acoustic in these installations. Nauman had swiftly transformed a practice that was totally personal and individual (for example, his solo performances for film and video) into one in which he created experiences that had physical consequences for the participating audiences. It is made clear in these works that an experience can be produced through a lack – in this case a lack of sound reflection in the normally highly reverberant art gallery environment.

Nauman himself has said of *Diagonal Sound Wall* that the idea of this work was 'the whole room being the sound, the whole room resonating, really locating the sound' (Simon 2004). The work was of course produced for the white-cube art gallery, a gallery that had been emptied of everything extraneous to the art object itself. The gallery walls, floor and ceiling were painted white, the windows covered over so that light from outside could not get in, so that the only illumination in the installation came from the bright unnatural lights that lit the space. In seeking to exercise a level of control over the spatial and luminous qualities of this space, Nauman's work furthermore seeks to address the problem faced by the artist working in the context of the white cube – for as we have noted, while these spaces are visually quiet, they can be very noisy – by controlling the acoustic properties of the gallery. In the white cube, sound bounces off the hard flat surfaces, amplifying everyday sounds such as footsteps, the gallerist's telephone conversations, coughing and so on. For *Diagonal Sound Wall*, Nauman placed a minimal sculptural form within the gallery and by doing so made it quiet(er). This work might then be understood as an intervention designed to further the development of the white cube's design, taking the isolation of the gallery from the everyday beyond merely the visual. Of course the contemplation of this particular work is not to be carried out by looking but by attending to the dampened acoustics of the room and the affect they have on the body of the visitor. Nauman thinks of this as 'manipulating the ambient sound that's in the room – a kind of sculptural manipulation of audio space' (Simon 2004). Nauman's empty soundless galleries, his sound-dampening installations, are then understood here to take the 'white cube' to its logical conclusion, performing an act of emptying that serves to further isolate them from the everyday. That is, the white space has had sound 'removed' from it, causing an audible quiet within the stark white space.

For Nauman, 'There is an immediacy and intrusiveness about sound that you can't avoid' (Simon 2003). His sonic interventions in the gallery do not stop with subtle sound dampening; one of his many parallel practices involved playing recorded or amplified sound into an empty gallery. In these works, sound is performative, vocal, at times non-linguistic (grunts and shouts), directional and aggressive. *Six Sound Problems for Konrad Fischer* (1968), for instance, initiated an investigation into recorded voice and sounds produced by Nauman that continues to the present.

For *Six Sound Problems*, Nauman, at the request of Fischer, visited Berlin and made a performance work on site, where sound recordings were made of the artist reperforming six earlier film works: *Walking in the Gallery*, *Bouncing Two Balls in the Gallery*, *Violin Sound in the Gallery*, *Walking and Bouncing Balls*, *Walking and Violin Sounds* and *Violin Sounds and Bouncing Balls*. The installation itself consisted of these recordings played on a tape loop installed in the gallery. Coosje van Bruggen, an art historian and critic, describes the installation as follows:

> On the first day of the piece, a visitor entering the gallery was confronted with a scene that might have been a stage set for a production of Samuel Beckett's *Krapp's Last Tape*; there was nothing in the space but a chair and a table, placed off center in

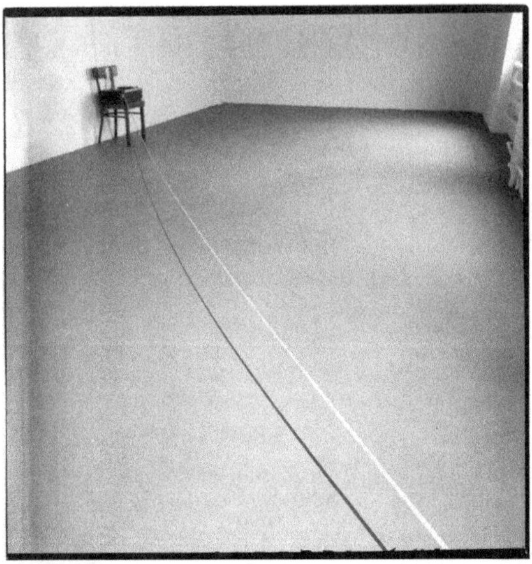

FIGURE 6 Bruce Nauman, *Six Sound Problems for Konrad Fischer* (1968). Courtesy of the Dorothee and Konrad Fischer Archive, Kunstsammlung Nordrhein-Westfalen, Düsseldorf.

> the room. On top of the table was a tape recorder playing the smallest loop of sound tape. On the following days, however, a visitor would find, strung diagonally across the space, ever-longer loops of sound tape, at one end threaded through the recorder head and at the other loosely around a pencil fastened to the chair with masking tape. (2002, 233)

Six Sound Problems makes the materials of recording (the tape recorder and audio tape) an integral part of the content of the work. While not as radical as earlier work produced by Nam June Paik, there is a nonetheless a certain resemblance here with a work such as Paik's *Random Access* (1963), which is made out of cut-up audio tape. Paik's tape cuts were attached to the wall, creating a 'drawing' from the magnetic strips, and subsequently played by the audience via a tape head that had been removed from the tape recording hardware.[6] *Random Access* exposes the material support of the technology, laying bare the gutted device. Paik can be seen to be radically deconstructing the playback technology, pulling it apart, while Nauman's use of the tape deck in *Six Sound Problems* does not damage it at all but rather recontextualizes the technology as a material of installation.

Six Sound Problems is formed from the all but empty gallery space of Konrad Fischer Galerie, the only material that could possibly be understood to be an art object is this recording media. A photograph of the installation shows the piece sitting alongside the gallery director's desk. We might imagine from this image alone that the recorder served some sort of administrative function, dictation perhaps. Something is not quite right, however, and suggests something more than this simple pragmatism since the magnetic tape has been drawn out of the tidily wound spool and pulled across the small gallery space. Not only has the tape been pulled from the spool, it is also held at length by a pen that is attached to a small white chair. As the tape plays, it winds its way out of the tape recorder and over to the chair with its makeshift spindle. The tape itself, drawn across the gallery floor, demarcates the space in a not dissimilar manner to the corridor works or *Diagonal Sound Wall*. To fully experience this work the audience must negotiate the tape, stepping over it to walk around the temporally sectioned off gallery space.

The audio that is played into the space explicitly draws attention to the presence of sound in Nauman's previous studio-based performances. These studio film works were produced in the period after he finished art school, when Nauman found himself spending a lot of time in the studio. At that time he did not have money for materials and, as his practice was not generally material-based, he lacked an obvious object-based workflow. These circumstances resulted in a situation where mundane activities (actions would be too strong a word here) he carried out in the studio developed into extended dance-like performance works. These activities took the form of repetitive tasks (such as throwing, stamping, walking around following a square marked out on the floor) in front of a stationary film camera. Other performances involved monotonous tasks, such as slowly measuring the space with his feet, making use of whatever was available to him – adhesive tape, balls and a violin he had recently purchased (but did not know how to play). Nauman performs these simple and functionless actions over and over, and while many of these works are soundless, those with a soundtrack include the everyday sounds that are formed from the actions.

The link to minimal music that is often made when discussing these works comes about due to Nauman's use of repetition and duration. Interviews with Nauman are peppered with references to music and especially to the New York-based composers of his generation, such as La Monte Young, Philip Glass and Steve Reich. Key to understanding the influence of these composers on his work is the use that these musicians make of duration and structure. Listening to their work, Nauman came to think about time and structure in an extended fashion. For example, he describes their influence in relation to the prolonged durational aspect of the video tape works:

> Videotape was really nice because it was a full hour, and that seemed to still imply you could get this same effect without having to make a loop. At this point I met Steve Reich in Denver, and then got to know him better in New York. Then I met Phil Glass. I also heard other music that Terry Riley and La Monte Young were doing. That was really important for me. I was able to use their idea about time as a really supportive idea. There was never anything you could really take from them, but their attitude about time and the things going on were very supportive. (Butterfield 2003, 174)

Alongside these young minimalist composers, Nauman was influenced by more established experimental artists and in one interview he namechecks John Cage, choreographer and dancer Merce Cunningham and the films of Andy Warhol, explaining that

> people (a lot of people) were thinking about how to structure time. John Cage was making different kinds of ways of making music, and Merce [Cunningham] was structuring dance in different kinds of ways. And then [Andy] Warhol was making films that went on for a long period of time. And Steve Reich and La Monte Young were making music that was structured in a very different way. So, it was interesting for me to have a lot of ways to think about things. (Art21 2001)

Clearly Nauman at this time was experiencing a lot of different things, but the key idea here is that he was being influenced by music, dance and film and all of these influences can be discerned in the work he made during this period. The influence of music, especially that of La Monte Young, for instance, can be heard in Nauman's record release titled simply *Record* (1969). Side A contains two violin tracks, which can be heard as a study in tonality through repetition and duration. As the artist was not a trained violinist, he simply performed the task (similar to the studio performances) of drawing the bow across the strings, creating a sound that has been described by Branden Joseph as resembling the violin work of Tony Conrad, a musician who earlier had often played with Young (Joseph 2008, 396 n.44). A major difference in approach between Nauman and Conrad comes from Conrad's sound being based on a highly tuned sense of pitch, while Nauman's sonic outcomes are based on the performativity of a rather mundane task.[7] On *Record* there is also a lengthy recording of Nauman's *Rhythmic Stamping (Four Rhythms in Preparation for Video Tape Problems)* that runs to almost twenty minutes. In this work Nauman's sparse studio becomes a container for the performances, the sound reverberant in the space. His large and rather empty studio might well be compared to the art gallery (this concept will re-emerge later in the book), as both house hard flat walls and a similar acoustics.

Room acoustics plays a crucial role in *Six Sound Problems*. By playing the performance recordings back into the gallery in which they were created, Nauman effects a spatial feedback loop. Van Bruggen alerts us to the fact that, 'This piece mixed recorded sounds with the natural noises of the environment' (Van Bruggen 2002, 232). The empty space of the gallery, in which the performances were recorded, is now an empty space in which the performances are replayed. The sounds that can be heard on the recording (and in the film/video piece recordings) are full of reverberation due to the emptiness of both the gallery space and of Nauman's studio. When these reverberant recordings are then played back in a gallery space, such as the Konrad Fischer Galerie, there is a double reverberation that occurs, a feedback loop. This can be usefully compared to Alvin Lucier's piece *I am Sitting in a Room* in which Lucier's voice is recorded to tape in a room and subsequently replayed and rerecorded (this will be discussed in greater detail later in this chapter).

Other works by Nauman of that time also employed seemingly empty rooms, which is to say galleries emptied of the objects that would generally be considered to fit within the taxonomic order of what can be classified as art, including *Get Out of My Mind, Get Out of This Room* (1968), *Touch and Sound Walls* (1969) and *Sound Breaking Wall* (1969). Like the installation shots of Michael Asher's works, existing images of these works serve only to document an empty space, the visual record hiding the fact that these works injected sound into the gallery from hidden speakers.

Get Out of My Mind, Get Out of This Room is installed in a gallery with only a single low-hanging light bulb in the room. A recording plays of Nauman repetitively reciting the title of the work in unhinged voices, at times quietly screaming, breathing heavily, speaking very slowly with pauses between words, the text at times almost sung. While being growled and grunted at, told to 'Get out of my mind, get out of the room,' the gallery visitor is in a quandary. Are they to follow the artist's orders? And if they do, how can they attend to the piece? The audience member has every right to be in the public gallery and would not usually think that viewing an artwork is a breach of privacy equal to getting into the artist's mental space. The visitor is faced with an empty gallery and in addition given the directive to 'get out', over and over again. The tension in this work is in part produced by the discrepancy between the desire to consume the work as it were, the fact that there is both nothing physical to be consumed and the continuous order to not stay in the gallery.

Touch and Sound Walls (1969), originally exhibited at Galleria Sperone in Turin, breaks with Nauman's intention to not allow his audience to make their own performance from his installations. The piece is the only work from this period that requires the sound content to be actually generated by the audience. For the installation, two walls are built 12 metres apart. The first has microphones placed behind it, while the second hides a set of speakers. When the wall is touched, the sound of the touch is played through the speakers on the other wall. The volume of the sounding wall was 'only loud enough to hear' and adjusted so that the 'amplified sound is the same kind of sound as the actual sound of touching and rubbing the wall' (Kraynak 2014, 154). For Jean-Charles Masséra this created an echo effect, identifying a slight time delay between the act of touching one wall and hearing the sound coming from the other wall containing the hidden speakers (2002, 185). The work can be read as being analogous with the video/corridor works, in which fleeting glimpses of the audience themselves are seen at the end of the corridors. In *Touch and Sound Walls* the audience hears a copy of the sound they have made here, now spatially displaced, which, as Marcia Tucker points out, 'effects sensory dislocation' (1970, 42). *Sound Breaking Wall* (1969) was installed in Paris at Ileana Sonnabend and likewise uses hidden speakers within a seemingly empty gallery. The piece utilized two walls in an L-shaped configuration into which speakers were placed flush with the wall and through which played two audio recordings: one of Nauman exhaling and the other of Nauman alternating between pounding and laughing (Sharp 2003a, 126). As with *Get Out of My Mind, Get Out of This Room,* this work plays with ideas of authority and space in the art gallery, interrupting the supposed sacrosanct quietude of the art gallery (even if this is, of course, somewhat of a misapprehension), questioning the right of people to be in these spaces. The abrasiveness of these works that use raised voices, what is more, serves an antagonistic function at the same time preventing the gallery visitor from being able to easily shut out the provocation. Kraynak points out that 'a viewer can typically walk away from an artwork and choose to ignore it or to not grant it a moment of contemplation, but when confronted aggressively by unwanted sounds that play regardless of whether one chooses to listen, such autonomy is circumvented' (2014, 160).

f Eternal music: La Monte Young

The white-cube art gallery, as we know well by now, is a reverberant space; the hard flat walls reflect sound and the lack of objects within gives sound free rein to bounce around. For La Monte Young this space presents a particular challenge but opens up an incredible array of opportunities to use this architectural feature to generate complex acoustic combinations out of simple sounds emitted into this space. His long-term project *Dream House* (1969–) plays sound into reverberant architecture at intensely loud volume, creating work that allows for what Young himself describes as 'listening inside sound' (Young 1965, 81). This is a break from the empty-sounding galleries thus far visited. No longer hushing the exhibition space, the compositions of Young employ volume to create a fullness of sound from minimal means, a composition that requires bodily engagement in order to fully experience the work.

Carrying out research for *Gallery Sound* on La Monte Young was an eye opener. I was surprised, if not shocked, by the lack of materials published on this composer. If this is so surprising it is in large part because Young has been so influential on the generations of minimal, drone and long-duration composers that came after him. He is also namechecked by many artists working with musical drones and long-duration installations, and he is regularly cited as influential by academics. In spite of this, there are only two published books with Young's name front and centre: *Sound and Light: La Monte Young and Marian Zazeela*, edited by William Duckworth and Richard Fleming and *Draw a Straight Line and Follow It: The Music and Mysticism of La Monte Young* by Jeremy Grimshaw. In addition to these books, there are a handful of chapters and discussions within books on minimal music, but even with these taken into consideration there is a real dearth of critical writing on Young, which becomes all the more striking when we compare the available material to the thousands of pages written about the diverse and expansive practice of Bruce Nauman, for example. One could of course posit that it is precisely because of the lack of diversity in Young's practice that there is so little written about him; his practice since the 1960s has been one of complete focus on the almost singular task of creating an eternal music from very few parts. Young's projects literally last for decades and it is then perhaps difficult for critics to have much to say about such a singular and minimal process. Whatever the reason, the result of this is that the importance of Young for the kinds of questions posed by the present volume has not been realized, and in order to redress this situation to some extent, this section of *Gallery Sound* will focus on Young's *Dream House*, a work that was first conceptualized around 1962 and continues to this day. If this work is so important for the questions posed here, it is precisely because it fills an empty space with a thick sound; the very design and nature of the composition requires us to rethink discourses relating not only to the role of sound in the arts but to installation practices also.

The *Dream House* is a unique work within the history of experimental music and is one of the longest running sound installations, and perhaps art installation, in the history of music/art.

The composition's scale is such that Young understands the piece to be a 'living organism with a life and tradition of its own' (Young and Zazeela 1996, 218). It is also unique as a musical composition in its installation, however, since it has, for the most part, been held within art contexts and has been supported for much of its existence by the Dia Art Foundation, which ultimately purchased the work in 2015. The *Dream House* sits in the fuzzy middle ground between music and art or, to put this differently and perhaps better, it sits as uncomfortably within the discourses of music as it does in those of art. The work that he produces remains in many respects alien to the context on which it is reliant while simultaneously alienating itself to a certain extent from the institution of music, which is to say the realm that would seem to provide the most natural fit for Young's work. Thus a composer such as Young finds himself taken more seriously by the art institution than by the institution of music.

In the 1960s Young and his partner Marian Zazeela began producing very long compositions. Long here should be taken to mean *really* long, with durations of days, weeks, months and theoretically for eternity. These durational works were initially housed in their loft apartment in Church Street, New York, where the pieces played day and night. In September 1966, after the dissolution of the initial version of the Theatre of Eternal Music (a group of which Young was a member alongside John Cale and Tony Conrad, among others, that composed and produced long-form compositions), Young and Zazeela quite literally lived inside the sound of electronically generated tones in what might be understood as a 'study' of the 'long-term effects of continuous periodic and almost-periodic composite sound waveforms on people' (218). If the anechoic chamber offers an environment in which people experience a certain kind of sensory deprivation, the *Dream House*, on the contrary, offered an environment for experiencing sensory saturation over extended periods. The use of sine-tone generators, first utilized in 1966, meant that the durational drones required for this experiment were not limited to the durational ability of a performer and could be simply left to run.[8] It was not only because the work was never actually turned off that it took on an eternal quality, however, as Young understood the series of sine tones and relationship between the tones to be eternal, meaning that when the piece was performed or when an electronic version of the work was initiated, any specific instantiation of the work was in fact only a continuation of the work, simply the work starting up again, taking up from where it had left off.

The first public presentation of the *Dream House* was at Galerie Heiner Friedrich in Munich in 1969 (Friedrich would later establish the Dia Art Foundation in 1973), and subsequently an array of 'short-term Dream Houses' were presented in the United States and Europe. These installations ran for durations of between four and one hundred days (219). In 1979 the work was given a semi-permanent home in New York city by the Dia Art Foundation at 6 Harrison Street, until 1985, when the space was closed. Subsequently the work was installed in nearby Church Street in 1993 where it continues to run as I write this. While there is no doubt that the work is a musical composition, it draws on and perhaps even initiated many of the tropes of contemporary installation. The Church Street environment, for instance, is painted entirely white, resembling an art gallery rather than a concert space for musical performance and listening. The space is saturated in colour by Zazeela's light installation and there are no chairs and no stage. The high volume of the work creates an all-over presence, making it impossible to identify any one particular area as a focal point, erasing the possibility of establishing any spatial hierarchy, any front or back within the space. The *Dream House* is electronically generated, rather than performed, employing a sine-tone generator to play sine tones that are very close to each other in frequency. Peter Blamey articulates well the ramifications of such a use of proximate tones:

> Using a pair of sine tones in a close ratio such as 64:63 to create a sonic environment emphasises one particular facet of listening inside a sound. While sustain would continue to be enacted through duration and harmonic stasis, profusion of sound is provided not by the number of components used to generate the sound or by the number of frequencies present, but by the acoustical and psychoacoustical phenomena produced by the two frequencies in the form of beats and standing waves. This shift has potentially significant implications for both the experience of listening inside a sound, and for defining what might constitute a sonic environment. (2008, 143–4)

La Monte Young has employed an array of different gallery-type spaces for the piece, including small independent galleries, experimental galleries and art museums. The use of art spaces was in all probability necessary simply for logistical reasons – while concert halls are set up for the purposes of concerts that run for a bounded period of time, Young needed installation spaces that would allow for the extreme extended durations of his works. Even more importantly, however, the architecture of the concert hall is not conducive to the acoustic effects sought in the piece, as Young required sound reflection in order to create the complexity of combined tones needed to generate certain psychoacoustical phenomena, something that would not have been possible in a concert hall designed to minimize acoustic reflections. Whereas the white cube is generally thought of as being an acoustically suboptimal space, here the empty rectangular room was far more effective than a concert hall in establishing and maintaining the wave patterns of the piece. Within this space, what is more, the audience for the work behave more like gallery goers than concert patrons, in part because of the nature of the space they are entering into, in part because they are given one rule when entering into the space, namely not to speak or make unnecessary noise. Once inside the audience can sit or stand and visitors are free to move around the space and to come and go as they please, leaving the piece to continue with or without their presence. On the occasion of my visit to Church Street, a small audience sat on the floor, one audience member doing some basic yoga while two others walked slowly but progressively through the room, most likely attuned to the changing wave patterns they experienced as their bodies passed through the space. The visitors who decide to walk around the space hear fluctuating amplitudes as they step in and out of wave forms, seemingly causing the volume to change. This freedom of movement has another effect, however, since by moving around, the audience member hears different acoustic effects:

> [Young's] use of constant sine or sine-like tones to realise the *Dream House* meant that standing waves – stationary vibrationary patterns formed by the superposition of reflected sound waves – became a structural feature of the work. The standing waves organised the sound into areas of high and low amplitude, meaning the balance between the relative volumes

> of the intervals became dependent on the physical location of listeners. Young would consider that this had the effect of making the listener's position and movement in the space an integral part of the sound composition, marking at least a slight recouping of the physical, embodied aspects of the listening experience that had been eschewed in favour of the internalised listening prescribed by Young's formulation of hearing. (161)

Any mention of Young's compositions from the 1960s onward will contain a comment on the loudness of the works. Volume allows for immersion of the body within a space made palpable by sound waves. The visitor to the *Dream House* actually feels the sound wave hitting their bodies, making them aware that sound is not only heard through the ears but also perceived through the body. Low-frequency sound waves vibrate the chest and stomach, causing the jaw to clench in an attempt to block further waves entering the mouth cavity and striking the teeth. This is not unlike the low-volume sine wave oscillations of Asher's La Jolla installation, except with the additional effect of high amplitude, in Young's installation. This use of high volume has psychological effects on the audience as we can see in the description of Steven Shaviro, an American philosopher and cultural critic, who relates the visceral experience of attending a performance of the UK band My Bloody Valentine, notorious for their ear-splitting live sound:

> It's loud, very loud. Swirling, churning guitars, aggressive distortion and feedback. Endlessly repeated, not-quite-tonal riffs. Blinding strobe lights. Noise approaching the threshold of pain, even of ruptured eardrums. This music doesn't just assault your ears; it invests your entire body. It grasps you in a physical embrace, sliding over your skin, penetrating your orifices, slipping inside you and squeezing your internal organs. You're brutalized by the assault – or maybe not quite. For beyond the aggression of its sheer noise, this music is somehow welcoming, inviting, even caressing. (2011, 120)

Shaviro describes the welcoming caress of this brutally loud performance, relating the feeling of near panic when first immersed within. Adrenaline is released and the fight-or-flight response is engaged, yet after a short time calm sets in and the body gives in to the experience, allowing it to enter. These types of reactions have been recounted numerous times and not only from My Bloody Valentine performances. The strongest sense of such feeling occurred to myself at a performance by Japanese noise musician Merzbow at the What is Music? Festival in Sydney. Merzbow is known for the extreme volume levels of his electronic noise performances. I was co-directing the festival in 2004 and this particular night was sold out with some eight hundred audience members in attendance. Merzbow played last and it was loud. Within the first few minutes (though I do not know exactly how long the feeling lasted) I was so panicked by the intensity of the sound that I felt it would throw my heartbeat out of rhythm. After a period, however, the fierce desire to remove myself from the danger subsided and was replaced with calmness, as if the noise musician was massaging my body from within, rubbing my shoulders and stomach. The volume of the music caused elation, calm and, most strangely, given the nature of the music which in terms of both volume and content could easily be considered to be aggressive, peace.

When music is played this loudly in live performance and in the installations of Young, the audience is forced into an individual, internal contemplation of the work. At this volume any social interaction must occur before or after entering the work, as to attempt to verbally communicate within the space is too difficult (and not allowed in Young's case). Alone with our thoughts we listen without speaking or talking, separated from others in attendance. Less poetically we could compare the experience of being immersed in audio while wearing headphones. Michael Bull has written extensively on the effects of curating your sound world through the use of headphones and portable media players, observing:

> The creation of a personalised soundworld through iPod use creates a form of accompanied solitude for its users in which they feel empowered, in control and self-sufficient as they travel through the spaces of the city. The disjunction between the interior world of control and the external one of contingency and conflict becomes suspended as the user develops strategies for managing their movement mediated by music. (2005, 353)

By filling the user's ears with music or podcasts, headphone use cuts out the sound of the external world, creating an inner field of contemplation from which to go about daily life. The experience of listening to sound through headphones while moving around has similarities to listening to very loud sound played through a sound system in that users are cut off from everyone else in their vicinity. In recent years there has been an emergence of headphone-only dance parties. Audience members don headphones and listen to the DJ's live mix, dancing as if in a regular club, yet anyone not wearing headphones hears no audio at all. The dancers move in seeming silence, in actuality no more cut off from others in attendance than they would be at a regular high-volume dance party. While perhaps now a trend, this practice originated as a pragmatic response to our contemporary lives in increasingly high-density urban environments, to prevent neighbours from hearing the music playing at parties and lodging a noise complaint.

In the case of very loud installations such as the *Dream House*, we then have a highly individual experience of a work. The experience is customized further by the individual listener's position in space, the amplitude of the sound being slightly different for each person as they move in and out of the standing wave's nodes. Here the logic of the white cube is turned in on itself as the reverential hushed art gallery is replicated in the very loud gallery. Silent contemplation is a requirement and gallery noise is kept at bay by the intensity of the piece. Where the art museum directs its audience to keep noise at a minimum so as not to disturb the contemplation of art by other patrons, in these loud spaces the quiet internal contemplation of the work is directed onto visitors. That is to say, the regular sounds that are always present within the art space cannot be heard – voices, coughs, air conditioning – nor can any outside sound be heard, such as aeroplanes, weather, traffic, New York car horns and so on. In fact, two of the problematic issues we have discussed in relation to the white-cube gallery and sound are in this piece either generative, in that the piece uses the reflective square-walled space to produce its desired effects, or no longer operative at all in the case of interference from sound sources either internal or external to the gallery, which are now entirely obliterated by the work.

In the performance of a musical composition, we usually expect to see the performance as well as hear it, just as in an art gallery we expect to see the visual artwork. Young has neither performer nor art object in the *Dream House*. While the very large speakers positioned in each corner may be black monoliths, they are certainly not installed as objects to be contemplated for their inherent aesthetic qualities. Young was an early instigator of this practice and numerous artists and composers have since worked with speaker-only art and music installations, placing a few speakers in the art gallery or a profusion of speakers in complex arrays, including Janet Cardiff, Francisco López, Susan Philipsz, Marcus Schmickler and Stephen Vitiello.

The installation of multiple speakers allows an audience to physically move around the gallery, listening to the multi-speaker sound systems from various self-regulated vantage points. The photographic documentation of such work merely draws attention to minimalist-looking speaker technologies and, of course, gives no sense of what is playing through the black boxes. An example of simply placing an array of black speakers in an otherwise empty gallery is German noise musician Marcus Schmickler's *Cubical Quad, Counting Lattice: Sonic ritual for nine loudspeakers,* inspired by Channa Horwitz's series SONAKINATOGRAPHY, installed in May 2015 at the KW Institute for Contemporary Art in Berlin. For this work nine speakers are stationed around the perimeter of a large white gallery; five of the speakers face into the space and four face the walls (so as to reflect off the walls). The sound content sits somewhere between voluminous drone created by simple sounds (similar to Young's compositions) and an electro-acoustic approach to multi-speaker composition (singular, spatialized sounds). At times the sound is loud and dense, causing perceptual shifts as the audience moves through the gallery, at other points voices and electronic sounds play clearly via individual speakers, positioning the sound discretely in the space. Using the large rectangular room's reverberation, the composition is designed for exhibition rather than performance and the audience in attendance treated the work no differently from any other loop-based installation within the art institute at the time. That is to say, they enter, walk around, sit, look out the window, plug their ears and leave between one minute and fifteen minutes after entering.[9]

Canadian artist Janet Cardiff, who will be discussed in more detail later in this book, has produced numerous installations in which audio speakers play a central role, both as a sound-producing technology and in literally placing sound within the exhibition space. Cardiff's installation *The Forty Part Motet* (2001) is an array of forty speakers placed in an oval around the perimeter of the gallery. The speakers play a rendition of *Spem in Alium* (1573) by Thomas Tallis, with each of the forty speakers representing the singing voice of one choir member. The audience can move around the speakers, listening very closely to an individual singer (something not possible in a live performance without offence), or they can position themselves inside the oval to hear the whole choir. Thus the gallery visitor wanders through the piece, free to pick their own listening vantage point and able to effect various combinations of voices during the playback of the piece. Cardiff and George Bures Miller's *Experiment in F# Minor* (2013) similarly uses multiple speakers. However, rather than using the kind of clean minimal black speaker boxes on top of black stands that have become relatively commonplace in the gallery setting, this work is a jumble of sizes and shapes, using an array of speaker cones freed of their boxy housing. The upwardly facing speakers play a guitar-driven indie rock song that track the listener as they move around the large table. This is made possible by triggering groups of speakers to play music as the wandering attendee casts a shadow on light sensors hidden on the table. It is a peculiar feeling to have the music follow you as you walk around the collection of speakers. Initially on entering the room, not having read anything about the piece, I was pleasantly surprised to find the playback of the composition following me around the table. Cardiff and Miller take their use of speakers another step further in *The Murder of Crows* (2008). In this work the placement of the speaker is designed to mimic the imagined position of where a sound event occurred. The squawk of a crow is played through a speaker positioned high up in the gallery beams while an instrument is heard being played from chairs where we imagine the musician sitting. A total of ninety-eight speakers were utilized to produce a theatrical installation, with speakers physically located around the gallery, placed on chairs, on ceiling beams and in an array that expands the usual understanding of the bounds of the exhibitable space of the art gallery.

g Echoing resonance: Alvin Lucier

Room reverberation is a central sonic element in all of the works discussed in this section of *Gallery Sound*, whether it is through the quietening of the room acoustics or the joyful deployment of the resonances in the room. While La Monte Young played very long and loud sounds into his empty spaces, Alvin Lucier in the late 1960s played simple, perhaps singular, sounds into a variety of rooms, including art museums, ballrooms, caves and the outdoors. His compositions allow for the differing signatures of the various spaces to play out and create new sonic experiences from performance to performance. Key to these works for Lucier is that the audience 'open up their ears to their environment' (1995, 66). As with Young, central to what Lucier found interesting in these spaces was their reverberance. Three compositions from the late 1960s, *Chambers* (1968), *Vespers* (1969) and *I am Sitting in a Room* (1969), were particularly involved with the use of reverberant spaces as both a container for sound and the 'instrument' for the creation of the musical content of the works.[10] These works do not specifically require an art gallery to hold them, but at the time many experimental composers were using art spaces for their performances for logistical reasons and also as the art institution was highly open to experimentation.[11] In these three works, Lucier makes use of the hard flat surfaces and the unforgiving echo of the empty-sounding gallery.

Chambers was composed after Lucier bought some conch shells that he then sawed off at the end to produce a wind instrument. Lucier came to understand that these objects were sound-making instruments (you could blow into them and produce a sound) and they were also containers for sound (sound entered the shell reflecting in it to produce a sonic effect that is likened to the ocean). He thought of the shells 'as small rooms that had resonant characteristics' (Lucier 2012, 87). *Chambers* started with these 'small rooms' inside conch shells, but was later expanded to include any hollow object that could hold a sound-making device. The eventual score comprises a list of resonant objects and a list of methods for making them produce a sound. When *Chambers* was performed at the Museum of Modern Art, New York, in January 1969, the performers brought various hollow objects into the art museum, including 'suitcases, boots, bags, lunch boxes, vases, pots, pans, and other small, enclosed chambers'. They also procured sound-making devices that could sound continuously, powered either by battery power or by mechanical means, such as 'toy airplanes, trucks, sirens, whistles, radios, and electric shavers' (87). The performers enter the gallery and are able to place their resonating objects anywhere in the room. Having been placed in and around the seated audience, the objects resonate not only with each other but also with the gallery, both individually and collectively. Lucier has said, 'I want to make the space be the interesting thing' (1995, 72) and here interest can be found in the sound of numerous spaces, large and small, resonating together.

In the late 1960s, Lucier turned away from employing traditional musical instruments, as were many experimental composers during this period, and rather than seek to expand traditional instrumental performance methods or extend the instruments themselves, Lucier looked outside of the normal purview of music for ideas. For *Vespers* the concept behind the composition came from bat echolocation. Lucier had read American zoologist Donald R. Griffin's book *Listening in the Dark,* from which he began to think about sound as waves rather than pitches, a critical and central element to his subsequent compositions (Lucier 2012, 81). As is often the case with Lucier's compositions, *Vespers* is heavily indebted to science, from which he draws inspiration. Crucially this approach to composition is never an example of the arts merely illustrating a scientific principle; rather Lucier's interest was in taking a scientific concept or knowledge and using it as the backbone of the work. For *Vespers* he gained access to a Sondol, a device initially designed to communicate to dolphins using sonar. The device functions by beaming brief pulses of sound onto objects, which are then reflected back to the user. The composition requires four performers to be blindfolded (the number of Sondols he had access to) and placed in four separate corners of the room. They are then tasked with moving towards the centre of the space using the Sondals to guide them. Without sight and with various objects placed in the performers' way, they must listen closely to hear their own echoes. It is important that they do not 'play' the device, in other words they should not attempt to reproduce musical rhythms or patterns from their performance, but rather carry out a process that makes sound only incidentally. Lucier describes the work as follows: 'A performance of *Vespers* gives you an acoustic signature of the room, as if one were taking a slow sound photograph over a long period of time. You hear what the room sounds like. That was mysterious to me and wonderful. It really turned me on' (82).

We all know that we sense our surroundings not just by looking but through a combination of all of the senses. A key mode of apprehending our physical space is through hearing it, from which we can determine a number of factors, such as its size and the materials it is made from (whether its surfaces are hard or soft for example). When our ability to hear a space is removed, we can feel isolated and disorientated, as occurs within an anechoic chamber. Barry Blesser and Linda-Ruth Salter point out that the sound of our footsteps on a wooden floor can relay information about the location of 'stairs, walls, low ceilings, and open doors' (2007, 1). A flat wall will echo a clap back to the creator of the sound event who can discern from various aural clues the approximate distance of the wall, its size and materials. In this way 'The wall becomes audible, or rather, the wall has an audible manifestation even though it is not itself the original source of sound energy,' as Blesser and Salter write (2).

They discuss the concept of 'aural architecture', succinctly summing up the concept as referring, 'to the properties of a space that can be *experienced* by listening' (italics in original) (5). Their ideal aural architect, therefore, would be one that considers the sonic properties of a structure in advance, and is attuned to how acoustics affect a space and its uses. This would then be incorporated into how an architect wants us to feel and how we are expected to act while in the space. However, for the art gallery, as has been pointed out, this kind of consideration has usually not been the case. Art galleries are almost always large, open, empty spaces and their acoustics are almost always reverberant (the exception being 'black box' spaces, carpeted and treated with acoustic rendering). In spite of their impoverished acoustic design, art galleries, as well as large halls and gymnasiums, actually provide the optimal conditions for the performance of *Vespers* because of their wide open spaces and hard flat surfaces, all of which are conducive to reverberation and long durations between sonic events and its echo around the room. The unpredictability of how sound will behave in such spaces is, in a very real sense, inscribed into Lucier's compositions that do not attempt to predetermine a precise outcome, giving very simple instructions to the performers who are free to explore the technology and the space. As Lucier puts it: 'I bring a very simple idea about a task that players can do and let the space push the players around'

(1995, 78). Interestingly it turns out that musicians are not the best performers of these pieces and Lucier often uses non-musicians (including school children) to perform his pieces because they do not try to make music out of the performance and are better at following the instructions without trying to add themselves to the process.

As an example, for one particular performance of *Vespers* at the Concord Academy for Girls in Massachusetts, four students played Sondols. Near the end of the performance Lucier handed out hundreds of tin toy 'clickers' or 'crickets' to the audience. As expected, everyone began to click them, causing the hall to resonate in response. Describing what he heard, Lucier states, 'The sound image of that room was marvellous. The room was being used as an instrument' (2012, 82). The sharp pulses of the Sondols were replaced with the diffused echoing of the clickers: 'The texture changed from one in which you could hear isolated echoes to one in which you could hear the room begin to ring or sing' (74). In a later performance in Helsinki, Lucier was, however, horrified when a music professor played a violin during the performance along with the 'clickers'. Perhaps Lucier should have followed Nauman's desire not to let the audience turn his work into their own performances, as this is clearly what happened here. The story does end on a positive note, with Lucier walking the streets in the early hours of the morning where he heard clusters of the clickers being clicked in the streets as audience members continued to experiment with them, listening to the echoes in the night air.

Clickers were also used towards different ends in American conceptual artist and gallery director Tom Marioni's *Sound Sculpture As* (1970) during the opening night's performance event. Arlo Acton performed the final work at the opening of the exhibition giving 'clicking crickets' to the audience. The audience fully involved themselves in participating during the performance, not just by clicking but also with plenty of talking, shouting and laughing. The raucous sound of the audience and the chorus of clickers was punctuated by Acton breaking a windowpane with a steel ball, an act that was greeted by loud yells and claps. After this dramatic event the audience persisted in their clicking throughout Marioni's announcement that the party was to continue at a bar across the road and, as he relates, they continued to click well into the evening (1970). The purpose of the clickers for Marioni's event was very different from that of Lucier in that Lucier utilized them in order to explore room acoustics, while Acton was more interested in creating a commotion. Of course both instances of the clickers' use do activate room acoustics but for Lucier this is achieved through careful exploration and for Acton through an exuberant celebratory atmosphere.

The resonance of large spaces becomes saturated with sound when echoes are produced in abundance. What happens, however, if a more singular sound, such as a human voice, was recorded in a space? And what if that recording was then replayed into the same space and once again recorded? And then that recording was played and recorded, and so on? The answer is that eventually the resonant characteristics of the room would begin to emphasize sympathetic frequencies within the vocal recording to the fore and simultaneously filter out those frequencies that do not resonate within the space. This is the basic premise behind one of Lucier's most well-known compositions, *I am Sitting in a Room.* While the work originally employed analogue recording technologies, it has continued to be one of his most often performed works even in the digital age, with new versions using programming and laptops or even smart phones to carry out what previously needed to be done via analogue and mechanical means. These new technologies, what is more, allow the work to be performed live, something that was not feasible when the work was originally composed. New digital technologies, indeed, have only increased access to this work, since students new to recording technologies are often tasked with recreating the work as a student project.

I am Sitting in a Room begins with the score, which reads:

> I am sitting in a room, different than the one you are in now.
> I am recording the sound of my speaking voice, and I am going to play it back into the room again and again until the resonant frequencies of the room reinforce themselves so that any semblance of my speech, with perhaps the exception of rhythm, is destroyed.
> What you will hear, then, are the natural resonant frequencies of the room articulated by speech.
> I regard this activity not so much as a demonstration of a physical fact, but, more as a way to smooth out any irregularities my speech might have.

Lucier wrote the text simply as an explanation of the process he was about to carry out. The language is descriptive and everyday as for him it was important that it not be poetic or overly aestheticized. If he wished the work to be imbued with this simplicity, this was because he wanted the listener to engage in the sounds that slowly developed from cycle to cycle and not to listen to the language itself. Whether or not he achieved this desire is contentious, and a number of critical readings of the work focus on Lucier's stutter itself. Christof Migone, for instance, argues: 'What this work performs is the transfer and inscription of the stutter onto the reverberant walls of the room rather than a genuine *smoothing out*' (2012, 137). However, Lucier himself was resolute that this piece was not about language but about music. He states: 'As the process continued more and more of the resonances of the room came forth; the intelligibility of the speech disappeared. Speech became music. It was magical' (Lucier 2012, 87).

I am Sitting in a Room is executed exactly as the script says. The score is read out and recorded, that recording is subsequently played back into the room and recorded again. This can be done as many times as one wishes. Lucier, for the first recording, did this fifteen times and much later, in 1981, it was cycled through thirty-two iterations for a recording released on Lovely Music. The initial version of the piece was recorded in his living room during the relative quiet of night time. Using two reel-to-reel tape recorders, each step requires that one tape recorder plays the previous iteration of the recording, while the second records the new one, a laborious task that necessitates that the tape be changed between tape recorders with every iteration. Each time the piece is produced it yields a very different iteration of the composition, but depending on the acoustics of the room this transformation can be swift or take many more iterations before the various reverberant frequencies of the space begin to reveal themselves.

The sounds that we hear in the later iterations of the piece are produced as certain frequencies of the recorded speech are reinforced when they match the resonant frequencies of the space in which the work is performed. Resonance is the reinforcement or prolongation of sound by reflection from a surface and is an important aspect of the propagation of sound in space. Anyone who has sung in the shower knows about resonant frequencies because when singing in a small enclosed space, certain tones sound more dynamic and more forceful, namely those that share the resonant frequency of the bathroom.

In discussing this work, Blamey eloquently describes the piece as delivering 'an intimate portrayal of the sonic possibilities contained in architecture as it explores the relationship of sound to space, enacted in the relationship of frequencies to dimensions' (2008, 198). This work is a process of experimentation whereby a known scientific effect, namely resonant room frequencies, is exploited to create a piece of music. The discovery of these resonant frequencies could be achieved more easily through various scientific methods, but for Lucier it is the process itself that is of interest. As Lucier puts it himself, 'I am not as interested in the resonant characteristics of spaces in a scientific way as much as I am in opening that secret door to the sound situation that you experience in a room' (1995, 98). What we hear produced by this process is the gradual transformation of the voice, from iteration to iteration, into a range of bell-like clusters of tones, some of which become louder while others fade into the background. The context is critical here and the composition draws our attention to our environment and the sound of the spaces which we inhabit. This is an idea that is evoked poetically by Lucier in a comment about *Chambers*, but it is a comment that could equally apply to *I am Sitting in a Room*. *Chambers*, Lucier says, is a piece in which he is 'trying to help people hold shells up to their ears and listen to the ocean again' (70). However here, instead of sound in a shell, an ocean fills a room.

I am Sitting in a Room cannot be produced without the use of recording technologies and as such it can be approached through a critical reflection of the recording technology itself, one that argues that what we are actually hearing is a composition that relies on its own mediatization. Greg Hainge posits that as one listens to the piece it is clear that we are actually not only listening to the resonant frequencies of the room but also 'the material qualities of both the recording and playback apparatus and the voice itself' (2013). According to Hainge, the recording process itself and the loss of quality of the voice in each subsequent recording play a crucial role in the production of the piece.

For my own purposes the critique of *I am Sitting in a Room* focuses on the composition and its recording relying heavily on the context into which it is played: Lucier's lounge room in the first instance, and the subsequent premiere at the Guggenheim Museum in New York on 25 March 1970. The original private context of the recording is conditioned by the very specific resonant characteristics of Lucier's home, while the premiere is situated in the public space of the art museum. The audience for the work heard the development of the composition generating tones at the various resonant frequencies of Lucier's living space being played back into a very different and more highly reverberant gallery space. As with *Six Sound Problems* by Nauman, we have a recording of a space being played back into another space, although instead of folding the same space back into itself, *I am Sitting in a Room* brings the acoustics of one space into another. This raises a question about exactly what the audience is then listening to when the audio recording is heard in the gallery and furthermore, as will be discussed in the chapter on Philip Glass and Steve Reich, it raises the question of why this musical composition is being premiered in the reverberant space of the gallery as opposed to the more conducive space of the concert hall.

However, *I am Sitting in a Room* also contains another reading, one that considers the way in which the resonance of a room has turned a communicable score into noise, the original meaning transforming over time into a sound that can be heard to communicate resonant frequencies while simultaneously destroying the original signal. In the following chapter, 'Noises in the Gallery,' the contemporary art space is heard to be already saturated in noises and sounds that are in excess of any artwork on display. Once the art museum has ceased to be a place of quietude, artists and musicians are free to make as much noise as they wish, so much so that we now expect a soundful experience when visiting a contemporary art museum, one that potentially sends us back out into the world not only with our minds opened (as has always been the case, hopefully) but also with our ears ringing.

2

Noises in the gallery

a The new loud art museum

In his book *Auditions: Architecture and Aurality*, Rob Stone, an academic in critical and cultural studies, investigates the notion of *askesis* (disciplined self-regulation) and argues that 'quiet, uninterrupted isolation' within urban planning as a strategy can be sacrificed in order to produce a social necessity, namely a social community (2015, 36). This statement has parallels with recent shifts in the perception of the art museum as a place for quietude and the quasi-religious appreciation of individual works of art. Instead, we find the art museum transformed into an architectural landmark designed to draw in large, dare I say uninitiated audiences, many of whom would not previously have attended exhibitions on a regular basis. Vast institutional art museums draw millions of people per year into their monumental architecture, each looking for an art experience that they share with many others. The size of the audiences for blockbuster exhibitions necessarily raises the noise floor of the venue. As a result, quietude and individual experiences of focused attention give way to a much larger social group who are not looking for the quasi-religious but, rather, for (art) entertainment. The good of the many outstrips the good of the few in these art tourism environments. Artists themselves have to deal with this new noisy environment and assess how to create situations in which these crowds can engage with their art in a meaningful manner beyond mere spectacle. This chapter will address these noisy contemporary art spaces. No longer are the artists discussed understood to be placing noise into the rarefied silence of the art institution; they are instead making noise in an already noisy space.

Art tourism at major art museums requires a new architecture and a new way of thinking about exhibition spaces. Art historian Reesa Greenberg points to a 'paradigm shift in the types of spaces used for exhibitions of contemporary art' between the 1960s and 1990s. She frames this as 'a move away from domestic-like structures to buildings associated with commerce and industry' (Greenberg 1996, 246). The small room-like gallery space, one that could be associated with a domestic environment in scale, complete with seating to enable patrons to contemplate the work on display, was replaced by the reallocation of former warehouse and industrial structures as preferred gallery spaces. The Tate Modern, opened in 2000, is a key example of such refurbishment, and many other art museums and art centres have since repurposed gigantic architectural buildings to create vast spaces for art. In his appropriately titled 'Art Factories', Wouter Davidts, an academic specializing in museum architecture, links the redevelopment of industrial spaces into museums to the smaller-scale repurposing of industrial spaces for artists' studios, which has a much longer history. Davidts suggests that this has or is believed to have a concrete effect on the art produced in these spaces. He writes, 'As much post-war art was created in lofts, many works were believed to be encoded with a sense of these spaces' (Davidts 2006, 29). For Davidts, these warehouse and factory conversions are thought of as having an aura of authenticity due to the patina of use set against the newness of contemporary art. The untouched walls and remains of industrial machinery are left to imbue the space with 'real-world' artefacts, creating a gallery that is far removed from the fabricated pure and clean white spaces of the white cube: this in turn imbues the art produced in and displayed in these spaces with 'real-world' significance.

This development has been international in breadth; in Sydney, for example, an abundance of industrial spaces have been refitted permanently or temporarily for the exhibition of art. The largest of these is an old shipbuilding site on Cockatoo Island, a small island in the middle of the Sydney Harbour. The Turbine Shop at the centre of the site is truly massive, containing some 1,700 square metres of floor space. Previously used to build ships, the space serves as the focal point of the Biennale of Sydney, but even the largest international biennale installations are dwarfed by the architecture. Artists have suspended cars, swung singing rocks and installed multiple speakers throughout the venue, but thus far all have fallen short when competing with the architecture. The most impressive in scale of the commercial galleries in Sydney that have repurposed industrial buildings was Anna Schwartz Gallery, formerly housed within the Carriageworks arts centre, an old railway building site. This was a vast gallery with some 347 square metres of floor space and a height of 6.5 metres. It required a unique approach to commercial art exhibitions, as domestically sized and framed artworks would be engulfed by the enormity of the space. Artists such as Marco Fusinato used the gallery to showcase large works destined for biennales or art museum collections, while the domestically sized works on sale remained in the smaller back rooms.

Reesa Greenberg's discussion of the shifting scale of the gallery and the use of industrial sites can also be directed at the many examples of light industrial buildings being converted into permanent commercial galleries, through to more temporary independent artist-run spaces. The latter is common in Sydney as artists take up residence in spaces that were previously used as laundries or sewing factories. These light industrial spaces typically have wooden floors, brick walls and many windows. On moving in, artists install temporary white walls, often placed to cover the windows. These alternative galleries have similar dimensions to art museum spaces, with high ceilings and large open rooms (far from the typical domestic space). These galleries in the hands of emerging artists are used for temporary, often experimental installations and, in Australia at least, for the most part they last only a very short while.

The showpiece of the expanded industrial space as art museum is undoubtedly the Turbine Hall at the Tate Modern in London. The museum itself draws tremendous audiences every year – in 2012–13 attendance reached 7.74 million visitors.[1] The Turbine Hall measures 35 metres in height, 23 metres in width and is 155 metres long. Since opening the museum in 2000 and up until 2012 the Tate Modern has commissioned one installation per year for its Unilever Series.[2] These installations are unique in that the artist is required to engage the vast exhibition space as a whole. In doing so they must ask themselves how they are to create something meaningful. Do they simply upscale their regular practice or just increase the number of objects on display? Or might there in fact be other ways to utilize the space that do not simply follow a 'bigger is better' logic? Davidts, writing in 2007, argued that, while all the Unilever commissions embraced the vast scale of the hall, 'none of them actually engaged on a substantial – i.e. semantic – level with the building, the institution Tate Modern, let alone the institution's broader cultural, economical or political context' (2008, 79). He later wonders 'what these works offered, besides an often undeniably spectacular and memorable art experience' (79).[3]

However, Davidts's commentary (intended as negative) does not perhaps take sufficient account of another crucial difference between the Tate Modern and the historical art museum, namely the audience. The audience entering into a space such as Tate Modern is radically different from the art gallery audience of yore not only in terms of size, but also in terms of who that audience are and what their expectations are. As Nick Prior observes, 'Today's audience descends on the museum with a more secular thirst for visual experience' (2003, 51). Instead of looking for singular visual objects created by genius, the audience is on the hunt for an experience, and this fact alone brings with it a whole host of shifts in how art is perceived. As Prior puts it, 'Aesthetic contemplation has been replaced by amusement, silence by bustle, education by infotainment, respect by relativism' (51).

In all of these commentaries there seems to be a feeling of loss for a previous time when art was sacred, unique and a thing that required education to be truly appreciated, a lament about the fact that art has become a spectacle and readily available for consumption, more an amusement park than a precious object. That art has become precisely this would seem to be what is suggested by Carsten Höller's Turbine Hall installation *Test Site* (2006). The work comprised five long metal slides that twisted down from upper floors above the hall. The works could be read as large extravagant minimal sculptures, but the requirement of use to activate them removes them from the lofty heights of precious objects. Children lined up to ride the slides as the art museum became a site of play. The art museum of old where children were to be seen but not heard was replaced with the noise of excited children awaiting their next turn. The question that needs to be posed, therefore, is whether the shift that has taken place in the way art has been received as it has moved into these increasingly monumental and spectacular spaces is actually something negative, something to be lamented, or whether in fact it is a symptom or driver of a more democratic approach towards art that seeks to broaden participation. Perhaps this is overly idealistic and one would undoubtedly need to ask what precisely is being experienced by the masses of children sliding down Höller's tubes: Are they having an art experience, or simply an experience? Is this the best time they have ever had in an art gallery or is there more to it? Did their parents bring them here for a revelatory art experience, or is this really the art museum as day care, with children left to play while parents drink lattes in the gallery cafe or peruse trinkets and designer objects in the gallery store? Whatever the answer, what seems certain is that the quietude and peacefulness of the museum is not to be found here nor is it likely to return any time soon, and anyone looking for an art experience removed and isolated from the everyday is out of luck.

The Tate Modern also has features now expected in any art institution, including a bookshop and a top-floor museum cafe that overlooks the river Thames. These facilities in themselves have very little to do with the consumption of art, but rather sit alongside the exhibitions and serve as a means to extract further funds from the visitor and also to keep them in the art museum. The concept that an art gallery can serve as somewhere one would want to stay beyond the purposes of an art experience demonstrates that the audience is now thinking of the art museum as not solely a cultural institution but as a site that serves multiple purposes.

Besides the extraordinary Turbine Hall, the Tate Modern also houses a series of exhibition spaces across its numerous floors that are not in any way contemporary. The remaining galleries comprise irregular white rectangular spaces and are of the form we most expect in a traditional art museum. This fact raises the question: Why is it that the dramatic Turbine Hall and its intensely contemporary installation programme is paired with a highly conservative series of galleries that display both the permanent collection and travelling exhibitions?[4] I feel that the traditional gallery spaces allow the art museum to carry out business as usual. That is, this part of the art museum holds what would have been traditionally expected and is furnished with exhibitions of the museum's collection alongside touring exhibitions. This allows the museum to put on display more extreme forms of contemporary art, thus drawing in its traditional audiences alongside a major new source of art patrons. The Turbine Hall is expansive and noisy but is beyond doubt the art museum's major draw card and as the next example will show the Turbine Hall and the installations housed within are what keeps the audience returning time and again to attend these major exhibitions.

In many respects the most successful use of the Turbine Hall thus far has been Olafur Eliasson's work *The Weather Project* (2003). Success here is ascertained across various measures, including attendance figures (some 2.3 million visits) and a use of the space that actually changed people's expectations of what art in an art museum could be. The project drew unprecedented crowds to an art museum. In images of the installation we can see people standing, sitting, eating, lying down, reading and chatting. The reason for this is the sun-like glow the installation created. In public talks I have given about this work I have joked that its success can only be explained by the British weather and that if it had been installed in Sydney it would not have garnered nearly as much interest. While a quip about British weather, there is an element of truth to it. In London people attended the exhibition time and time again, many returning daily to eat lunch in the installation that bathed this entire, cavernous space in a warm glow that contrasted sharply with the crisp, harsh light of the London winter outside. As James Meyer aptly describes, 'The museum is not so much "revealed" as transformed into a destination, an event' (2004).

The installation of *The Weather Project* consisted of a large sun-like sphere created with hundreds of lights and a haze machine. Light filled the hall with a yellow orange glow and massive mirrors were placed on the ceiling, adding an element of self-awareness to the audiences' interaction with the work. Eliasson's work caused the noise floor of the museum to be substantially raised as some two million people came to experience the piece over its duration. Its diverse audience broke numerous edicts of the art museum – both explicit and implicit rules of museum decorum. On entering the hall one could not expect to have an individual and internal experience of the installation; instead, the audience had a group experience. For example, there is an image that shows a group of people lying in various formations, observing the patterns that they made collectively in the mirrors overhead. In more ways than one, the strictly regimented space of the museum and in particular its quietude is not simply contravened but comprehensively desecrated and irrevocably transformed by installations such as this. But if we can surmise from this that institutions such as the Tate Modern (in its Turbine Hall and new extension, at least) can truly be understood to have fully embraced a new direction for the contemporary art museum, a crucial question is raised for our consideration of the place of sound in the gallery. Indeed, if silence has now been eradicated from the art museum, what is an artist to produce now that they are free from the once-imagined silence of the visual artwork?

One possible response to this question can be found in Bruce Nauman's Turbine Hall installation *Raw Materials* (2004), a sound piece that had little or no visual element, for which Nauman drew together twenty-two audio works that spanned the length of his career as an artist. Set in the expanse of the massive hall, Nauman did not attempt to fill the hall with sound, a feat that would require a stadium-sized sound system and levels of sound exposure no public servant would be expected to endure. Instead, he placed flat directional speakers (coincidently resembling minimal paintings) down the length of the hall with sets of two speakers facing each other that played the same work. Due to the directionality of the speakers, the audience walked in and out of bands of sound associated with one work before entering into another (Dexter 2005). To experience *Raw Materials* the audience was required to walk the length of the hall while listening to four decades of practice – and to do so with no visual cues. The use of the vast space of the hall for sound that was projected directionally was successful in that the audio was not required to compete with the surrounding noises within the space and instead the work sonically occupied sections of the hall that could only be heard while standing in proximity to the speaker. Thus the noises of the expansive gallery were kept out of the work while the work itself was bounded by the directional speakers' focused area of sound.

b Intervention and interference: Marco Fusinato

Nauman's work engaged a vast expanse with sound, but the work itself did not produce noise within the gallery; instead, by employing directional speakers sound was contained and perhaps tamed. Not all artists have responded to the changing landscape and architecture of the art museum in this way, however, and many artists, in response to the shift towards an art entertainment industry, have sought to create installations capable of engaging large crowds by filling the gallery with sound. One example of this tendency can be found in Australian artist Marco Fusinato's work that often uses excessive volume (such as in the work *Constellations* previously discussed in the Introduction). At times this can be so excessive that it crosses the pain threshold, becoming an investigation into what level of noise can be pumped into the art gallery while still being supported by the art industry itself.

An earlier volume-based work, *FREE* (1998–2004), asks similar questions of an entirely different environment. The work takes the form of a series of performances that consisted of Fusinato entering guitar shops and testing instruments, as he describes: 'I'd walk into the shop, press record and ask to try a distortion pedal, that way they'd have to give me a guitar and an amp. I'd then proceed to play at high volume until I thought I reached the threshold' (Fusinato 2015).

A roughly produced video of one of these performances exists, in which we see Fusinato in a guitar shop ostensibly shopping for guitar pedals. The guitar shop, located on a busy street in Auckland, New Zealand, allows clients to try out the merchandise, including a large rack of guitar effects pedals, all neatly lined up. *FREE* is a performance work in the space of the music shop, and it tests what can be done in the retail environment, utilizing guitar performance techniques well outside of what is normally expected from those trying out musical equipment (usually endless recitals of 'Stairway to Heaven'). In hand-held footage of one such performance (the only video recording of the series) we see an example of Fusinato's signature guitar style, using effects and feedback to generate noise. To those who know about noise music, Fusinato is certainly playing music with the equipment, but this is not anything like the music that would usually be played by potential customers trying out equipment.

In *FREE*, Fusinato pushes at the limits of what kind of sound can be played in a specific context and at what volume, and much of the work that he has produced in the art gallery context follows this same methodology in order to interrogate the boundaries and limits of what is possible in gallery spaces. Within this practice three distinct approaches can be teased out: extreme volume in installation, durational noise within music performed during gallery hours and silent noise. These approaches intervene in the presumed sounds allowed within art galleries, they impinge on the quietude expected by patrons and they often sound out over the top of other works exhibited (something already discussed as a troublesome element of works with an element of sound, however, in this case they do not merely interfere but completely drown out the sound of other works in the vicinity). What is at play here, however, is not merely a strategy to get people to pay attention to one's work in the increasingly noisy and crowded space of the contemporary art museum, for the deployment of noise within the music and art of Marco Fusinato represents a critical investigation into the proper use of gallery space, the art museum as a public venue for entertainment and the threshold of noise.

If, as I have argued, the development of art spaces into massive venues for entertainment has raised the noise floor of the gallery substantially, ending in effect the expectation of the art museum being a place of quietude, then the space is ripe for experimentation with noise and volume. The contemporary art gallery is already filled with sound emanating from the artworks and from the crowd gathered to have an art entertainment experience. How does a contemporary artist contend with the lack of quiet? It is almost inconceivable to think that a work based on silence, such as Nauman's *Diagonal Sound Wall (Acoustic Wall)*, could survive within the contemporary gallery environment today. The attempt to dampen the sound within the gallery would have to contend with the sounds of the contemporary gallery and the desired acoustic experience would be lost within the daily goings-on of contemporary exhibition practices. One response to the noisy art museum is to make work that is in excess of the raised noise floor. In the case of Fusinato this excess is extreme to say the least, and it is in a very real sense this new context for art that gives Fusinato permission to take the volume of sound within his work to new heights.

Fusinato delivers a shocking art entertainment experience for gallery visitors and anybody who happens to be within the vicinity of his work. Warnings are placed nearby to make sure attendees are not shocked into cardiac arrest from the explosive noise that his work generates. For *Constellations* – the work that was the opening example of book, for which the exhibition visitor was tasked with hitting the central wall with a baseball bat – this wariness reached extreme proportions as gallery invigilators were at any time able to silence the sounding wall using a remote device. This addition was designed to allow the gallery staff to control the brutal shock that could have been caused to the unwary patron who entered the gallery unaware of the possible sonic assault. Fusinato tests both his audience and the art institution itself with these disruptive works, asking how much entertainment they can handle. In terms of the art institution, they are faced with a high-profile artist whose works cannot help but cause noise complaints both from within the bounds of the gallery and beyond. Noise emanating from the Artspace installation of *Aetheric Plexus* in 2012, for instance, led to the Biennale of Sydney, whose offices were above the gallery, demanding that the work only run between 5:00 and 6:00 pm, leaving a silent but threatening installation for the remaining opening hours.

Aetheric Plexus, originally produced in 2009 for the Australian Centre for Contemporary Art in Melbourne, displaces entertainment equipment, including a concert sound system and theatre lighting, from its expected role of highlighting a performer to redirect it towards the audience itself. The work includes a lighting rig that produces 13,200 watts of white light and a PA that plays bursts of white noise as loud as 105 decibels. As visitors enter the gallery space, they see lying on the floor before them a stage lighting rig, its multiple shiny metallic stage lights facing them. The quietude of the gallery does not last long, as the audience member entering the space, in Fusinato's words, 'triggers an intense environment of white light and white noise, one that simultaneously delivers both violent and ecstatic experiences. I'm interested in the critical discourse around the gallery and museum shifting from a place of contemplation to one of entertainment. When activated the blast … turns the audience into performers as they are forced to deal with the onslaught' (Fusinato 2015).

It must be said that the experience of the work is extreme, even on multiple viewings of the work being triggered it still causes a jolt to the heart. The lights emit heat that is felt at the same time as the 105 decibels sound hits the body in an intense experiential moment. The audience seeking entertainment certainly have an unexpected experience, their heart rates raised by the experience much like it would be by the thrill of a rollercoaster ride. The work also critiques the expected norms of gallery space in terms of sound, as the volume is very loud for the briefest of moments and it noisily reverberates into the adjoining spaces, through the ceiling and out into the street.

In a later installation, entitled *Aetheric Plexus (Broken X)* (2013), the already large sound system was taken to its logical end point, as a line array was installed in a gallery. A line array is a column of identical loud speakers that are generally used for large music venues and outdoor festival stages, not for gallery sound. When the audience enters the gallery, the banks of speakers and lights in the unexpected setting instantly threaten them.

More than simply an art installation, Fusinato's work operates oftentimes as an intervention that mounts an institutional critique. This critique is affected by the disruptive behaviour of the piece itself but also by the discussions that it elicits at the heart of the very art institution itself. When a gallery decides to stage a Fusinato exhibition, curators, technical staff and other artists exhibiting work all enter into a discussion behind the scenes over precisely why Fusinato requires a line array and how loud it will actually be.

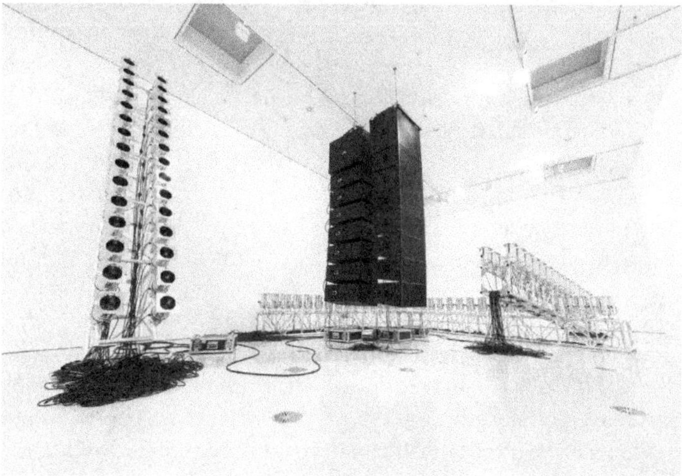

FIGURE 7 Marco Fusinato, *Aetheric Plexus (Broken X)* (2013). Courtesy of the artist, Anna Schwartz Gallery and the National Gallery of Victoria, Melbourne.

It is certainly the case that many of those involved will not benefit by the installation of his work as the sound emanating from the installation is disruptive to the everyday goings-on of the gallery and also to any sort of remaining quietude within the neighbouring galleries. The continuous jolt to the office work at the heart of the Biennale of Sydney offices above Artspace or, in the case of the earlier installation at the Australian Centre for Contemporary Art, who originally commissioned the piece, and the requirement that gallery staff be subjected to these blasts throughout the day, could well be argued to have caused stress to all those affected. The very fact that this work has been installed attests to the consultative power of the artist and his critique of the development of art entertainment via the use of entertainment tools themselves.

Intensifying the use of high volume a step further by combining it with duration, Fusinato's work *Spectral Arrows* is a series of performances for which he plays noise music in the art gallery for extended periods. The work is durational, with the artist entering the gallery as it opens to set up his sound equipment before playing at extreme volume until just before the gallery closes, allowing enough time for him to pack up. The work is performed in his signature drone/noise/feedback style and, of course, at very high volume. *Spectral Arrows* is not contained; the music screams out at a fearsome volume, filling the gallery with noise that spills out into adjoining spaces. The piece was performed at Artspace, Sydney, where Fusinato's exhibition The Colour of the Sky Has Melted (2012), a survey show of the artist's work, was on display. I entered the gallery a number of hours into the performance to see Fusinato performing while facing *Double Infinitive 4* (2009), his back turned to the audience who were sitting and standing around the space. The performance is confronting, especially for any casual patron hoping to immerse themselves in a more normal sequence of protocols and quietly contemplate the exhibitions on display, since the extreme volume of Fusinato's noise music allows no escape. Occasionally *Aetheric Plexus*, which was installed in the neighbouring gallery, would blast out slightly louder than Fusinato's noise performance. The work is resolutely not normal art gallery fare and requires the audience to ask itself how to consume a performance of this duration and extremity. Should one treat it like a video piece, ducking in and out like most do, or should one stridently stay for the full duration? Does the work actually expect or require such commitment from the audience, and if so what changes if the audience does not stay with it in this way? In answer to these questions we could look to La Monte Young's *Dream House*, as audience members cannot possibly stay for the duration of the work (it is eternal), but other than being told not to make unnecessary sound, his audiences are left to their own devices. While I was visiting the work I watched a person do yoga in the space, while a couple slowly walked around the room holding hands. In Fusinato's case a key element of the performance is that the spectacle he has created cannot readily be consumed in its totality; it is possible to do so but for most it is not a serious proposition. Therefore, the audience can come and go as they wish and due to the volume of the performance this action does not cause the same type of distraction as if patrons of a sit-down music concert decided to come and go from the concert hall.

In terms of audience exposure to durational performances and video works, two pieces from 2010 are comparable to *Spectral Arrows*: Marina Abramović's *The Artist is Present* and Christian Marclay's *The Clock*. The former work required the artist to be present at the Museum of Modern Art, New York, from 14 March until 31 May continuously during opening hours. The audience is able to move freely around the edge of the large gallery in which the artist was installed, as it were, and they were free to come and go as they pleased. There are accounts of audience members who spent many hours attending, hoping to join Abramović at the table she was sitting at, and stories of others who returned day after day, even though, unlike Abramović, they were free to leave and not return.

Christian Marclay's *The Clock*, meanwhile, is a 24-hour-long piece in which every minute of the day is displayed through the sampling of an image of the exact time from a film. The clocks in the piece are also aligned with the actual time of the day, so at 10:35 you will see a clock showing 10:35 from within a film. The work, as with *Spectral Arrows*, allows for the audience to come and go as they wish and to stay as long as they desire, as the work remains open to the public for the full twenty-four hours. There are anecdotal accounts of people attempting to watch the full piece from start to finish and, unlike *The Artist is Present*, it is entirely possible that an individual could in fact do this.

Both *The Artist is Present* and *The Clock* adhere to the expected decorum and edicts of art gallery patrons. Audience members for *The Artist is Present* were asked to not touch Abramović and during gallery hours there was a reverential hush among those who were in the presence of the artist. The installation of *The Clock* at the Museum of Contemporary Art, Sydney included plush couches arranged to face the big screen, much like an extra comfortable cinema theatre and, as with Abramović's work, the audience kept their voices down while watching the durational video piece.

To fully consume a performance of *Spectral Arrows* would be to comprehend it in its entirety, subjecting the body to the aural assault for six or more hours. Would such dedication actually add anything that is not accessible to those in the audience that stay for thirty minutes, or even less? The duration lends a fetishistic aura to the work as Fusinato creates something only a few can apprehend in its full excessive duration, and perhaps only a few would actually want to. For the general audience the piece is difficult, it is literally hard to experience, the sound hurts in a fashion that is only appreciated by a small number of people (noise music enthusiasts). To experience the work for any length of time is to put yourself inside the high-volume performance that could cause damage to the non-earplug-wearing audience member.

Conceptually noise is difficult to pin down, perhaps as it should be. For noise theorist Paul Hegarty, the perception of noise occurs in relation to a historical, geographical and culturally located subject (2007, 3) and 'Noise also has to contain judgement: it is "unwanted." Can noise be wanted – clearly that would define the noise in question as not-noise' (Hegarty 2001). Noise as unwanted is critical here as no matter how hard the art institution tries to control the work of Fusinato they will fail. This is crucial to understanding Fusinato's intervention, as the artist becomes more successful he can ask for more, but by asking for more he literally creates a situation in excess of any institutional framework.

There are numerous other examples of sounding interventions into gallery space and, while not as intense as the 120 decibels roar purported to be unleashed onto the audience for *Constellations*, of equivalent intent is Thomas Zipp's use of large bells. Zipp installed a large bronze bell, originally meant for outside use, in the Boros Collection housed in the Bunker Gallery in Berlin. Visitors are able to enter an area above a small double height gallery and ring the bell by pulling a rope. This action, unsurprisingly, causes an extremely loud bell sound to resonate throughout the building, literally sounding across all levels of the gallery. If one is inside the same gallery as the bell when it is rung, the sound is deafening. When I visited the gallery the attendants were mindful of the work, making sure visitors did not pull the bell too often and checking if people were in the space below before allowing the bell to be rung. In the same manner as Fusinato's intervention, Zipp's bell acts not only as a sounding artwork or simply as an interactive artwork, but also operates on the level of an institutional critique. By placing this extremely loud sounding object within the frame of a gallery, the structures that support the everyday running of the space are stretched. The invigilator must allow the bell to be rung (this is not a visual artwork), but in allowing it to be activated by an audience member the invigilator (generally charged with maintaining the calm and decorum of the gallery space) actually allows for an intense intrusion on all of the spaces of this private art gallery.

c Condoned noise

Social sounds within the walls of the art gallery are of course not always the content of an artwork. More often than not these relational sounds are caused by the everyday goings-on within the day-to-day business of the art gallery and are more likely to be considered noise than an artful experience. Galleries obviously contain art, but the contemporary art space houses many other things, such as cafés, a bookstore, lecture theatres, a museum library and staff offices. Events such as high-profile artist talks, exhibition opening night drinks and live music performances draw large social crowds. As Duchamp already told us long ago, however, in the art institution anything and everything is ripe to be made into art. The exhibition tour, the public talk and the party atmosphere of the exhibition opening celebrations have all become opportunities for artwork, mostly in the form of performance art, to occur. Understood as interventions, these works might be impossible to ignore or could completely fly under the radar of many of those present.

The general expectation for hush is forgotten when the art space becomes a social venue, such as during an exhibition opening. At this time the gallery doors are thrown open and patrons enter the gallery with drinks in hand, loudly discussing art world gossip. The space is filled with people networking and socializing at what is a key public event of any exhibition, yet the noises created make attending to the artwork impractical. The exhibition opening is certainly the worst time to experience an exhibition – unless the opening is the actual exhibition – as contemplation and focus are stunted by the desire to network and the often extremely high level of background noise. In terms of artworks that employ sound, the opening makes any attention to their sonic output almost impossible.

An opening, then, is a noisy affair with larger than normal numbers of visitors within the reverberant space, forcing them to raise their voices so as to be heard above the noise floor of the event. Take for example the exhibition I curated entitled Mistral at Artspace Sydney in 2006, which consisted of four sound works that forego amplification (discussed in more detail below). Two of the works were for the most part silent, while the other two had extremely low-level acoustic sounds. The opening was exceedingly busy and it was impossible to hear the works or for the audience to ascertain if the art had sound or not. The works' sound was so far below the noise floor of the opening that they stood no chance of being heard and because of a lack of amplification, the gallery staff could not simply turn the volume up on them. The opening in all its cacophony silenced the exhibition.

Artists have responded to the noise levels at opening events in different ways: some intervene in, and add to, the noise by performing loudly, while others place their work quietly under the noses of those in attendance at the busy event. Canadian artist Diane Borsato's work is an example of this surreptitious interventionism. Her work *Falling Piece* (2010) employed six dancers who, over the course of an opening, staged a series of falls. The dancers were dressed in accordance with the dress code of a gala benefit party held at the Art Gallery of Ontario and over the course of the performance they deliberately fell, as if slipping on the unstable floor, some one hundred times. These falls were witnessed by the two thousand guests and the performance itself was not announced in any way (Springgay 2012, 84). Another work that exploited the opening setting was entitled *Cloud* (2012); in this instance, however, twenty-four participants wore highly fragrant gardenia boutonnieres to an opening. The twenty-four flowers were enough to fill the entire space with scent and for an hour these participants remained in the gallery, creating a 'cloud' of fragrance before they quietly left the building.

At the other extreme is the work of performance artist Kusum Normoyle who, on the opening night of Sound Full, performed in front of Fusinato's colossal mural. Normoyle is known for her interventions into gallery openings, alongside similar interventions in public spaces and within music concerts. In her work the opening becomes a site for performance as a massive wall of noise emanating from guitar amps and a physical and aggressive performance style temporarily replaces wine sipping and gossip. For this particular performance she set up two guitar amps in the gallery in front of *Reproduction of Double Infinitive 2* and, at an undisclosed moment during the evening, let loose a churning mass of screams and feedback of immense proportions. I use the term 'churn' very deliberately as the feedback that filled the three-storey-high atrium seemed to swirl around the museum above the heads of the unsuspecting audience. The sound generated by the large open space's reverberation further reinforced the sounds emanating from Normoyle's brand of pre-linguistic screams, hisses and mouth sounds.

This type of noise was not expected in the calm and reified environment of an art exhibition opening and the members of the champagne-sipping art set present were unprepared for the four long minutes of extreme sound pressure that they were subjected to. For a brief moment the two works came together, intervening in the expected norms of the museum environment. Fusinato's mural creates a silent noise within a sound-filled exhibition, and Normoyle's dark screams and roaring feedback sees the female body caught in a maelstrom of volume and physicality. While we might be able to shut out the sounds of Fusinato's riots by simply turning away, there was no way to escape of sound of Normoyle's performance that night.[5]

The opening then is always a contested site, it is a celebration of an exhibition, but one in which attention to the exhibition itself is made difficult by the social sounds created by an enlarged audience who attend the event as much to witness the exhibition itself as to support the artist and be a part of the atmosphere of the event. Social sound is critical here, as within recent art this relational aspect of the art institution has been brought to the fore, to become a live practice that fully embraces the chattering sounds of a community that leaves behind the hushed environments of the art museum.

d Social sounds

Of course, conviviality did not begin in the Turbine Hall of the Tate Modern, nor is it confined to the well-meaning art patrons who attend invite-only exhibition openings. Socially engaged art practices are a recognized feature of contemporary art, especially since curator Nicolas Bourriaud coined the term 'relational aesthetics' in 1996. The quintessential installation that aligns with Bourriaud's relational aesthetics is probably Rirkrit Tiravanija's *untitled (free) 1992/1995* (first shown 1992). The installation consisted of tables, chairs, a refrigerator and other kitchen utensils in a gallery filled with people eating, creating a scene that resembles a dinner break in the middle of an installation rather than an exhibition opening. Gathered in the space, people ate bowls of rice and Thai curry prepared by Tiravanija. Using the communal experience of eating to enact a socially engaged situation, Tiravanija created a work in which the content is equivalent to the social dynamics of the opening event. Thus, this is not an installation that should be understood visually, it is a series of unrecorded conversations held over food. In socially engaged practices, the sounds created within the art gallery – people conversing, the clicking of chopsticks, the clink of bottles placed on tables – form not an unwanted noise but the productive hum of social interaction. Each sound can be heard to symbolize a relational outcome that has been situationally produced by the artist.

These practices rely on the social and are not in any way attached to the individual art piece or the individual art spectator. By the turn of the century, the art gallery was regularly filled with the cacophony of voices, discussions and very un-art-like events in the name of art. Within these practices the noise floor of the art gallery was substantially raised as socially engaged art works almost always involve the sounds of conversation. Social sounds reached ethically questionable heights in the work of Santiago Sierra, whose interventions in the gallery have 'employed' workers, beggars, prostitutes and drug addicts to carry out often degrading tasks for little more than minimum wage. For *160 cm Line Tattooed on 4 People* (2000) at the El Gallo Arte Contemporáneo in Spain, Sierra hired four prostitutes who were asked to allow a single line to be permanently tattooed on their backs for the equivalent price of a shot of heroin. In the documentation of the work the prostitutes are seen facing the gallery wall. The footage has no soundtrack, but an animated conversation between the women can clearly be seen as they laugh and talk among themselves. These voices would have reverberated around the gallery space, joined by the loud buzz of the tattoo gun.[6] By not including a soundtrack to the document, Sierra effectively silences the four women who, while certainly being exploited by the artist, seem to be enjoying the experience that has taken them out of their everyday reality.

Sound is critical to the relational aspect of these practices; the murmur of conversation is framed by social or institutional settings, yet as with my previous discussion of the photographic documentation of artworks, sound is not made available in most of the archival record. For example, most of the documentary footage available on Sierra's meticulously furnished website does not include sound. We can see in a work such as *9 Forms of 100 × 100 × 600 cm Each, Constructed to be Supported Perpendicular to a Wall* (2002) that there is some interaction between the African American workers who hold up large sculptural rectilinear columns and also the audience members conversing with each other in the gallery space, yet we cannot hear anything that is going on. This silence gives the work a sombre feel, as if it is done very peacefully without interaction from the participants or the spectators, but this is undoubtedly far removed from how the piece would have felt to those who could hear it. What is more, the sounds of the discussions that were had between the gallery administration and job centres over the transaction and the nature of the proposed work are not included in the documentation either, and a critical element of this relational work is thus kept behind closed doors. The silent documentation of *9 Forms* also hides a radical gesture enacted by people hired to hold up the beams at the opening, which they refused to do, questioning the lack of dignity of holding the pillars at the opening. 'At such a moment, the human positioned as support for the art object refused their undercounted position; using the time-based capacity for alternative action, they altered the social situation by walking out of it and, in doing so, questioned the givens of "social conditions that allow [Sierra] to make his work"' (Jackson 2011, 71).

Shifting from a relational situation where conversation is critical to a practice that closely attends to very small sounds and imagined sounds, Japanese experimental artist and musician Akio Suzuki creates situations for his own listening, a contemplative creation in which Suzuki is not so much a sound maker as a sound listener. Suzuki has two practices, one that employs instruments that have been built by him and that are played in a concert environment and the second, which is of interest here, that I consider a listening practice. This is not to say that Suzuki is necessarily an especially good listener or a highly trained listener, but, rather, that the medium of the work *is* listening. Suzuki often does not make anything that specifically creates a sound, rather he builds or finds situations from which he listens and in the process he becomes a listener to his own listening. This concept can be illustrated with a work entitled *Hinatabokko no kukan* (Space in the Sun) (1988). Set in the Tango region of Japan, close to Kyoto, Suzuki constructed two large parallel brick walls from 10,000 bricks he had made by hand. The construction, which took two years to complete, comprised a large square floor area and two walls that faced each other. Once the project was completed, Suzuki sat between them for a full day on 23 September 1988, after which, I was told, he abandoned them to nature. Describing the experience he recounts: 'On the day of the solstice, I sat by the center of the northern wall and was immediately bitten on the neck by several mosquitoes – it was an unexpected way to begin. In order to make my many supporters proud, I applied my entire body and soul into this moment – an irreplaceable experience in my life' (2012).

The work itself cannot be simply understood as a sculptural environment even though it resembles a minimalist sculpture in form. Rather what Suzuki has built is a listening situation that is intended for his own listening only. Chris Kennedy describes the piece as illustrating 'the idea of building a space for the privilege to listen unabated to the natural world. With it, Suzuki claimed a space and directed his own listening. Although *Space in the Sun* is in disrepair, it still exists for sonic pilgrims who want a space for their own listening' (Kennedy 2013).

In photographic documentation of Suzuki's works he is often seen calmly in the act of listening. Sitting or standing he smiles at what he hears in environments he produces or discovers, environments that seem to have been created solely for his own listening pleasure. *Hinatabokko no kukan* was not built to be experienced by anybody else and its remote location makes it difficult for any 'sonic pilgrims' to visit, but his other works are accessible to an audience who are invited to experience the places that he has discovered and that he has listened to. These more accessible works are not created in an attempt for the audience to emulate or to live his experience; this is not a didactic lesson on how to listen to some particular thing. Rather his work is about or has been created only to allow for his own listening and the situations he produces do not require any other audience than himself.

Suzuki's work *Economical Music* (2006) is an installation of long lengths of timber lined up over a number of wooden pallets to form a very large musical stave that is missing any notation – that is, the score is blank. Placed around the installation are twelve chairs from where he or the audience are able to listen. There is an image of Suzuki sitting in the installation, listening and feeling good in the process of his own listening (Licht 2007, 130). In the fashion of John Cage's *4′33″* the visitor can experience an 'economical music', one that does not require instruments nor recordings; rather, the music is formed from the sound heard within the gallery.

For the *oto-date* (Sound Place) (1996–present) series, Suzuki stencils a circular pattern on the ground. This pattern is formed from a stylized depiction of two ears that can also be seen as forming a footprint onto which the listener stands. The symbols used for *oto-date* are stencilled directly onto the ground in a range of different situations, including on bridges, closely facing a wall, in a quiet garden, on a busy street corner, in a quiet underground tunnel and in a watery puddle. As a grouping they form a type of sound walk, with a map of their location being provided to the walker who traverses familiar or unfamiliar ground looking for the marks indicating the aural vantage points from which to listen. The process feels somewhat like an orienteering exercise, with the walkers looking closely at maps, and also at the ground, hunting for the symbols. These marks are positioned across an area of the city and their placement seems to indicate that this precise location holds some specific interest for Suzuki in relation to the sounds that one hears when standing on the symbols, but precisely what this interest might be is not spelt out for the uncertain listener. It could be a sound produced by the wind in the trees or it could be an effect elicited by the passing traffic. It is not important exactly what Suzuki heard, something we can only hazard an uncertain guess at, but rather what the subsequent listener hears.

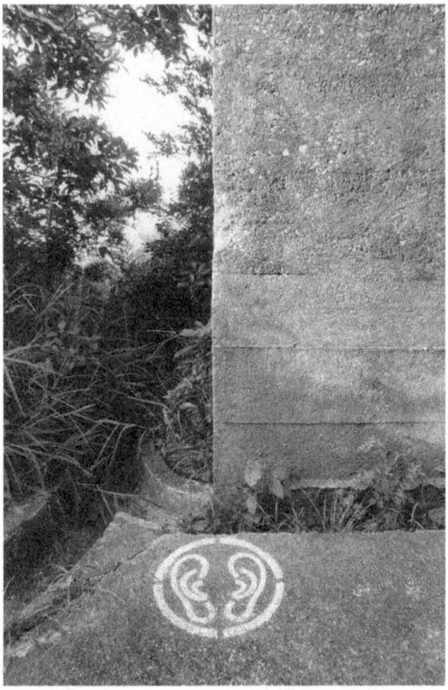

FIGURE 8 Akio Suzuki, *oto-date* (1996–), photograph taken on site for the *Around Sound Art Festival*, Hong Kong, 2010. Courtesy of the artist.

In 2006 I curated an exhibition entitled Mistral that developed from the experience of having Akio Suzuki as a guest at my sound-focused art gallery Pelt. I had spent a few days with Suzuki and, during and after his performance, I felt a certain lightness. Suzuki's performance work involves eliciting sound from found and handmade objects and instruments, including glass pipes, rocks, small flutes and a device made from two cans and a spring. The latter instrument is not unlike the child's game of making a 'telephone' from paper cups and a length of string. Around that time I felt that there was a developing fatigue caused by continued exposure to amplified audio not only in the often highly amplified concert situation but also throughout the day, from the bedside alarm to the car radio, stereo and TV. Away from the stress of amplification, it was a relief to listen to acoustically produced sounds, and Suzuki's practice thus seemed to me to be music to make us hear again. The curatorial premise for Mistral was to produce an exhibition and a series of performances for which no amplified sound would be present. As such the curation of the exhibition paid close attention to the exhibition space, opting for a series of works that, in line with Suzuki's influence, made little impact on the sound environment itself.

New Zealand artist Philip Dadson's installation *33rpm"UV/R#2 (Rock Records)* was made up of a series of circular discs made from photographic paper that were affixed to a large gallery wall. The discs themselves are Dobson spectrophotometer charts and visually resemble compact discs with a rough pattern created by Dadson rubbing pigment onto the discs after placing them on rocks that were deposited by volcanic eruptions. Thus these discs are a visualization and imagining of a historic and catastrophic sonic event, the sound of which has long dissipated, creating a monstrous noise that can only be imagined.

Vicky Browne's installation *Calling Occupants* (2006) also, for the most part, produced very little actual sound. Various bric-a-brac lined the walls, 'records' made from twigs and silver coins, domestic objects turned into phonographs, a cardboard box gramophone, roughly made wooden cassette tapes. Listening to these objects involved imagining the sound they could make and reflecting on the nostalgic memories they elicit. All of the works on display thus demonstrated the central conceit of Mistral, namely that attention to small and imagined sounds further reflected on the nature of the gallery experience. Not wanting to add to the amplified sounds that we are forced to hear in the everyday environment, the exhibition tried to create an environment in which the ears of the audience were given space to listen and imagine (im)possible sounds.

While previously Marco Fusinato's works have been discussed in the context of loudness and intervention, he has created score-based compositions that are imagined as explosive noise works. Since 2007 Fusinato has produced a series of compositions entitled *Mass Black Implosion*. These works are formed from the scores of avant-garde compositions onto which Fusinato draws a straight line from every note (or equivalent mark) on the page to a single arbitrary point on the page to form a dark vortex or singularity. When the compositions have many notes or are graphic scores with many points, Fusinato's resulting 'composition' is dense and dark, as the mass of lines converge on a single point. When the composition has a smaller number of notes, the artist, following the system put into place for the creation of the series, necessarily intervenes less and the 'composition' is less dark. Brandon Joseph has explained that 'each "implosion" implies a new version of the score as a noise composition, all the notes melding into a simultaneous cacophony of indeterminate duration' (2011, 194). This is to say that to play the work the performer is asked to play all of the notes at once, an action that would create a terrifying noise. Given the difficulty of doing so, however, the performance of these scores remains always within the realm of the imagination as the audience observing these works must imagine the mass of sound that would be created if these works were being performed.

These works by Browne, Dadson, Fusinato and Suzuki sit silently in the art gallery, acting more like drawings and sculptures than sound works, yet they add to the sonic imagination of the audience in attendance who hear sounds that are activated by their presence. However, whether the sounds imagined are from a distant past, a catastrophic event or are contemporary sounds that are on the edge of audibility, what connects all of the works in *Gallery Sound* is the very literal bodily presence of the audience and the simple act of walking. The final part of this section on noises in the gallery will pay attention to the everyday and often unnoticed act of walking in the gallery.

e Walking and listening

Walking is a physical motion that connects two places, where we are now and where we will be in the foreseeable future. It is something every day, not necessarily the stuff of interesting tales or deep philosophical questions (although both may occur to the walker in and around a walk), especially if the walk is very common, such as from the train to work. Of course walks can also be a leisure activity, taken on a sunny Sunday afternoon, perhaps alongside the harbour foreshore. Walking is considered here as an everyday practice that is critically addressed by disparate disciplines that have integrated the very act of walking into their forms of knowledge creation and learning.

In his research on walking in l'Arlequin in France, professor of philosophy and musicology Jean-François Augoyard discusses walking as an intermediate practice, describing it as seemingly 'unremarkable and hardly of interest' (2007, 19). Yet, as he writes, 'One and the same trip can summon up the private and the public, the individual and the collective, the necessary and the gratuitous' (19). Augoyard found social implications in the tracks people walked during the course of their day, the decisions that were made and the detours taken. Thinking about walking in the context of this book, it becomes apparent that we cannot experience the kind of art talked about here without in some way walking or moving around the gallery. We wander around the art gallery, perhaps knowing it very well and thus navigating our way via well-habituated routes, or, alternatively, when visiting new or unknown art venues, encountering every different space with a constant sense of exploration and discovery, never knowing what to expect from room to room or even from gallery to gallery.

Walking is a multi-sensory practice: the walker experiences their location through all of their senses all of the time. We cannot think about a walk without thinking about the sights, sounds, smells, touch and, to a lesser degree, the tastes (perhaps we are eating an ice cream, for example) that accompany any such displacement through space. From the feeling of the weather to the mechanically induced sensations caused by the surrounding traffic, from the bright colours of the autumnal leaves and hay-fever-inducing spring flowers to the sounds of the trees and the life that happens in and around them, walking is a highly sensate experience and one in which we learn much about our environment. Learning about our environment while walking is critical to the type of walks that are commonly presented within urban space as an introduction to their history, culture, landmarks and geography. These urban walks have been appropriated by artists as a way of transforming the official narrative given to a particular place, such as the Dadaist practice of touring boring and ugly areas of the city (with no one actually in attendance), the Situationists following the psychogeography of a city through their *dérives* (wandering without a specific plan), and contemporary practices like locative gaming (games played with mobile devices) and sound walks, both occurring in urban environments. All these walking practices take a known and mapped urban environment and challenge what we expect and think we know about it. The sound walk is an aural practice, where a group walks through the environment paying close attention to the sounds experienced. Here walking and close listening are the two modes of experience that this audience is directed to pay attention to. Over the course of the walk the intention is that the sound walker hears afresh the surrounding environment and in the process turns from hearing the everyday sounds that surround them to *listening to* these sounds. By paying close attention to sound while ambulating through an environment, the walker discovers and learns things from the sonic environment and also begins to notice different types of sounds and the way they interact with each other.

Within the gallery, walking would seem to allow for mobility in the engagement of works, yet in many situations we are rendered immobile as the dominant form of artistic objects in the art gallery, namely still or moving pictures mounted onto the wall seem to invite us to stand immobile before them to contemplate them. The exception to this is, of course, sculpture or installation works that are placed in the centre of a space, in which case we tend to walk around or even through them, but even here the works themselves stay put. In the black cube, meanwhile, we sit on benches, facing forward and watching the action occurring on the screen in a manner more akin to the posture we adopt in the cinema. Similarly, media-rich installation might include a set of headphones that require the audience to stand still while wearing the device. Thus, while there is a sense that we are free to amble around an art gallery's exhibits, we are, more often than not, encouraged to place ourselves within designated areas and to attend to individual artworks from within a strictly delimited space and posture.

One method of keeping the gallery patron in place is the use of didactic panels. There is a good chance that while in the art museum you will be interested in learning something about the exhibits. The museum has developed a range of strategies for the dissemination of officially sanctioned knowledge around its collections and displays, the most obvious of these being the didactic panel – the small rectangular board placed alongside an artwork that delivers information such as the artist's name, the title of the work, the year it was made and so on. The panel might also give an explanation or a reading of the artwork itself, in the process linking it to the curatorial vision of the exhibition. Alongside these panels, many exhibitions have a curatorial introduction to the exhibition as a whole, a much larger and more expansive text, often filling an entire wall at the entrance to the exhibition, which lays out the overarching themes and concepts. When such curatorial statements are present, the audience reads about the exhibition they are about to enter and is made aware of its aims before experiencing the work. What connects these two modes of knowledge transfer is the requirement that the audience stands to read them, perhaps within view of the work or alongside it.

Sound works, as has been discussed, are not tied down to one place (except perhaps when, as they often are, played through headphones attached to the gallery wall). By escaping the bounds of the gallery we are often able to hear the sounding work well before we arrive at the space in which it is located and, what is more, hear it transform and modulate as we approach ever closer to that space. For instance, when attending an exhibition opening for *A Lot of Sorrow* (2013) by Ragnar Kjartansson at König Galerie in Berlin 2015, I could clearly hear bass frequencies throughout the refurbished St Agnes Chapel (a brutalist concrete church originally built in 1967 and subsequently transformed into a gallery). Walking up a staircase the sounds grew louder before the bass rhythms revealed themselves as belonging to American indie rock band The National's well-known song 'Sorrow'. Walking into the gallery was a surprise and a joy, as the soaring architecture forms an exceptional space. Huge and cathedral-like, the sound of the video work filled the gallery and reverberated around the hard, flat concrete and wood structures. In this particular installation the work is projected at the end of the long space, leaving the audience members to scatter themselves throughout it, walking around the gallery, listening to and watching the work from a variety of different vantage points, turning the whole experience into a mediated and meditative concert. In the context of this particular installation the work becomes massive as it fills the space with the sound of 'Sorrow', and as there is only a single visual element within the gallery, no other works compete for our attention. This was a vastly different installation of the work to a previous one from the same year at Artspace in Sydney. In the case of the latter installation, the work was a small part of a group show, tucked away in a corner of the gallery. The projection and the sound itself were not grand and there was nothing about the architecture of Artspace that added to the work. In the case of the König Galerie, I learnt about the work through wandering, my walking led me into the massive space and I learnt about the sounds I could hear from downstairs through the pace of my steps as I ascended the staircase and entered the vast gallery. I also learnt about the work by moving through the exhibition itself, looking at the work, listening to the sound and experiencing the architecture from different angles.[7]

This case study tells us something about the embodied gallery visitors who congregate in this deconsecrated space to watch and listen to the work. The installation is not only played at a relatively high volume, but the voluminous architecture creates an expansive and full sound work. The embodied audience, in their gallery wandering, listens to *A Lot of Sorrow* while also listening to the remodelled St Agnes Chapel and its reverberant architecture, which in turn reinforces the audio track of the installation.

What this experience exemplifies in an exaggerated form is that when walking around an art gallery one is never focused solely on the art itself; rather, the artwork's expressive qualities are always necessarily entangled with the space in which it is exhibited – and this is not nearly as apparent when one stands motionless before a work. The sonic nature of *A Lot of Sorrow* actually encourages the patron to engage and experience both the artwork and the architecture of the space through movement. Like sound, the visitor is not bound by an artwork to one spot but is spurred on to move both through and between spaces, experiencing the work from multiple vantage points.

There are a number of institutional methods that take the mobile bodies of their patrons into account and allow the visitor some mobility while they learn about the works on display. One example is the gallery tour. Much more than the noises made by individuals or small groups of friends walking through the spaces of the art museum, the gallery tour introduces sounds into the art gallery that impinge upon the quiet gallery environment. Sounds such as the educated voice of the docent leading the tour, the questions from the people on tour and the hushed background discussion between friends intermingle with other unintended sonic effects of the group tour including footsteps, excited chatter between works and so on.

The guided tour as an institutionally sanctioned constituent of knowledge transfer has been exploited by artists who have 'appropriated the guided tour in the manner of a "strategic inhabitation"' (Drobnick 1995, 31). Peggy Phelan points to an imperfect imitation that creates excesses and gaps, allowing for multiple and resistant readings (32). Andrea Fraser in particular engages with the concept of an imperfect imitation in a series of works for which the artist took on some of the tropes of the tour guide and intervened in the expected norms of that role:

> It was not intended to distinguish a particular body of work as new or as a substitute for any of the labels at that time in use, from 'institutional critique' to 'post-studio art', 'site-specific art', 'context art', 'community-based art', 'public art', the more generic 'project art', or the even more generic 'cultural production'. 'Services', rather, was intended to identify one aspect of many, but not all, of the practices described with those terms: the status of the work, or labor, of which they consist and the conditions under which that work is undertaken. (1997, 111–12)

Fraser describes this as a strategy that allows artistic labour that is not specifically associated with a product to be accounted for, in this instance, the gallery tour. Fraser created a docent character by the name of Jane Castleton who led gallery tours for the work *Museum Highlights: A Gallery Talk* (1989). This ambulatory talk was anything but a straightforward guide, as Fraser incorporated slips of the tongue, digressions and ramblings into her presentation, as well as inappropriate remarks (Drobnick 1995, 34). By acting in a manner those on the tour would not have anticipated, the artist brought to their attention the expected norms and edicts of an employee of the art museum. Just as in the noisy interventions of Fusinato, this artistic tactic creates a tension between what is expected and what is actually delivered and, in doing so, frames our assumptions about the role of the institution and how we consume art within the bounds of the art museum.

Beyond didactic panels and gallery tours, the third mode of knowledge transfer commonly made available by the art institution to the art patron is the portable audio guide. At the entrance to most major art museums visitors have the option of taking a pair of headphones and a portable sound player to carry with them on their visit. Portable information systems were first used in a museum context in 1952 at the Stedelijk Museum in Amsterdam, taking the form of 'Short-Wave Ambulatory Lectures' (Tallon 2008, xiii). The museum's audience walked through the museum carrying a receiver and wearing headphones, and in doing so they moved in and out of reception of short-wave transmissions that broadcast information about the various artworks in close proximity to them.

Obviously the technology of the audio guide has radically changed in the intervening years, but the basic concept remains the same. Audio guides allow the museum audience freedom of movement while they receive information about various exhibits, artworks and points of historical interest. Many find these audio devices to be more useful than, or simply preferable to, the gallery's other educational strategies, either because they can stand directly in front of the work and view it while hearing about it or else because they allow individual freedom to stop and start the tour at will – unlike museum tours led by docents. Generally, the audio guide is a dissemination of the official story the institution wishes to represent, and it is no more or less so than the didactic panels, exhibition catalogue or gallery tour. While content-generating companies are now employed to produce these increasingly sophisticated audio productions, their job is to represent the institution and the knowledge it holds through its collections.

Holger Schulze suggests that the adoption of the audio guide by the museum visitor with its soundtrack and headphones, 'expresses a certain negation or even rejection of architectural space' (2013, 198). While Schulze gives a highly speculative account of the use of the audio guide, he raises a valid point here, namely that the sound space of the museum itself (the present space for the visitor) is often vastly different from that experienced through the headphones. The soundtrack might be recorded in the actual museum space, or, conversely, in a voice-recording booth and as such the user hears multiple sound spaces over the course of the tour. The use of official audio guides by the museumgoer allows them to enter a sonic environment that is situated outside of their presence in time and space. That is, they listen to narration, music and sound effects that are not part of their present physical space. As a result, the audience explicitly engages in purportedly 'visual art' through senses other than sight. By physically moving around the museum space and having a bodily and aural experience in front of the art on display, the audience gleans information and understanding of the distant visual object in a much closer and more intimate manner, led by a voice that speaks into their ear as it directs them to objects of interest, perhaps while music plays soothingly in the background.

Alongside the audio guide produced by the museum, unofficial guides made an appearance in the early part of the twenty-first century with the development and popularization of the podcast. A front-page article in the *New York Times* entitled 'With Irreverence and an iPod, Recreating the Museum Tour', discussed, in a rather shocked manner, the phenomenon of unofficial podcasts created by college students being made available to the public as a free download (at the time the official museum audio guide cost USD5). The reason for the tone of the newspaper article was that the official institutional knowledge created by the prestigious art museum was being undermined in these satirical, unsanctioned guides. Museum audiences would be given information about the work that could not be verified and, in the case of the student guides, was humorous and not at all appropriate for an art museum. Freely available through the downloadable podcast, the sound of irreverent students entered the gallery via the back door of an uncontrollable source.

The article also made reference to the practice of 'sound seeing', which, according to the author, involves narrating one's travels onto a recording device and subsequently uploading the recording to the internet. However, these unofficial audio guides resemble sound seeing in that the creator cuttingly narrates their tour of the art museum, describing and explaining the artworks and then making this tour available online. The term 'sound seeing' is a rather strange idea in itself (as, of course, you cannot see sound) and also the act of 'sightseeing' always includes hearing the sounds as one tours places of interest. This practice, and the article itself, points to the invasion of yet more sound and noise (both the sonic noise and informational noise) into the art gallery environment.

In a manner similar to the artistic intervention into the realm of the guided tour, artists have also capitalized on the audio guide, finding it ripe for exploitation as an artistic practice. For example, for *La Visite Guidée* (1994), Sophie Calle arranged a series of her own personal items within a museum and created an audio guide that related personal stories associated with the objects. Andrea Fraser created an audio guide *UNTITLED (An Introduction to the 1993 Whitney Biennial)* (1993) that focused not on the artworks in the exhibition but rather on the staff within the art institution. Her audio guide scripted interviews with the museum staff in which she asked the staff questions about the museum audience, creating a guide that rather than elucidating the collection turns its attention to the gallery patrons themselves (Fisher 1999).

Janet Cardiff in particular is known for her audio walks (discussed further below) but has made only a small number of walks that take place within the space of art museums, including *Chiaroscuro* (1997), which was produced for the San Francisco Museum of Modern Art. Cardiff notes that the art museum 'posed some challenges in terms of dealing with a fairly consistent, boring soundscape and a limited amount of space'. Cardiff is hearing the spaces of the art museum against a practice of hearing outdoor urban environments with their multifarious combinations of volumes, timbres and noises. In contrast, the ambient sound within the museum environment is, as she points out, overtly uniform and predictable. Of course it is my contention that sound within the gallery is always present and that it is complex in character, yet Cardiff's assertion could be understood as devaluing the complexities of sounds in the gallery. We should understand her comment in context here: that is, the sound she is hearing outside is dynamic and full of discrepant sounds, wind, birdlife alongside traffic and social sounds. Thus, when designing her gallery work, there was a lot less sonically interesting (to her) or perhaps less by way of sonically diverse spaces to be utilized.

As with her other audio walks, here Cardiff works with narrative to prescribe a series of stories to the walker. Leading the listener around the museum, the audio instructs them to stop at various points to consider a series of what could be referred to as imagined memories: imagined because the museum at the time was newly built (opening in 1995) and thus these memories could not have possibly have occurred within its architecture.

Outside of the gallery, as mentioned above, sounds shift around much more than in the relatively controlled environment of the art gallery, the exterior 'soundscape' then being for the most part more variable and complex than what we find within the architecture of art spaces. Before continuing the discussion of the audio walk (via the sound walk), there is a need to understand some of the discussion behind the concept of the soundscape, especially in terms of the soundscape outdoors and its relation to the soundscape within the gallery. Canadian composer R. Murray Schafer is credited with conceptualizing and explicating the concept of the sonic backdrop as the 'soundscape'. So, for example, while we are inside the gallery we might expect a very particular kind of soundscape, one that recedes into the background where it should go unnoticed. Yet a soundscape is a constant presence that, in many situations, slips out of our attention and then back into it through our day. As a domain of investigation, Schafer posits that, 'The soundscape is any acoustic field of study' (1993, 7). If we take Schafer at his word, then all possible fields can be apprehended as a soundscape, from a rainforest to a domestic kitchen, from a black metal concert to a secluded beach. For Schafer, this research is to be developed around 'sounds that matter', and conversely it will be 'necessary to rage against those which don't [matter]' (12). These 'sounds that matter' are to be found in the 'natural' soundscape, and therefore have not been polluted by industrialization. Thus a key element of Schafer's notion of the soundscape is the drive towards an 'acoustic ecology', an area of research that studies 'sound in relationship to life and society' (205). This is a discipline that requires the researcher to be on location in order to experience the effects of sound on the living creatures within it. According to Schafer, to discover the sounds that need to be encouraged, potential 'soundscape designers' will need to develop their listening through a process of 'ear cleaning', and by doing so they will come to respect silence (205). In Schafer's vision, from the ground zero of silence, the future 'acoustic designer' will be enabled to make the correct decisions when designing our 'soundscape environments'. This is something that clearly cannot be accomplished from inside a laboratory (or a studio); instead, the researcher must venture into the field.[8]

Schafer's ideas have been highly influential on subsequent artists and composers who work experimentally with sound, especially those interested in sourcing 'natural sounds' to use as the content of their work. It is useful to be aware, however, that the term 'soundscape' is often used in contexts not covered by Schafer's initial delineation of the term. Emily Thompson, for example, begins her book *The Soundscape of Modernity* by directing our attention to Schafer's use of soundscape environmental concerns (2002, 1). However, given her interest in modernist technological development and urban architecture, it is important for her to distance herself from Schafer's strict definition of the term as most of what she is explicating would fall into his undesirable sound category. For Thompson, via French historian Alain Corbin, a soundscape is, 'an auditory or aural landscape' (1). This definition relies on the assumption that a landscape can be apprehended through the non-visual senses and allows for the understanding of the landscape being made available through all of the senses.

Anthropologist Tim Ingold takes issue with any notion of the soundscape. He points to the use of the term as a tactic to direct attention away from vision towards sound. This in turn leads us away from all of the other senses per se by overly focusing on the aural (Ingold 2008, 10). He argues:

> A symptom of this manoeuvre is the multiplication of 'scapes' of every possible kind. If the eyes return the world to us in its visual image, conceived in art-historical terms as landscape, then likewise the ears reveal a soundscape, the skin a touchscape, the nose a smellscape, and so on. In reality, of course, the environment that people inhabit is not sliced up along the lines of the sensory pathways by which they access it. It is the same world, whatever paths they take. (2011, 316)

Thus the term soundscape does not resolve the issues set up by the notion of a landscape dominated by visuality by deliberately sectioning off a single sense, that of hearing. Of course the term 'landscape' is not itself inherently visual and thus replacing 'land' with 'sound' does not somehow hold an equivalence in terms of the senses. That is, as Ingold argues, we do not have touch or smell scapes, but we also do not have visual scapes or light scapes.

Beyond the inherent problems of focusing on one sense in this manner, Ingold declares, 'Let me begin by explaining what the landscape is not. It is not "land," it is not "nature," it is not "space"' (2000, 190). Ecological theorist Timothy Morton, for his part, argues that a sonic history (a history that is formed around the audible past and that is the sonic equivalent of a pane of glass on the frame of the landscape painting), 'aestheticizes place, as the suffix "scape" warns us. A landscape is a painting. A soundscape has been framed. It implies distance. There is a sonic equivalent of a frame or a pane of glass separating historians from the time they are evoking' (Morton 2007, 95).

Furthermore, Morton points out, what delineates a given soundscape are the aesthetic decisions about what is included and excluded. Both soundscape historians and composers decide what constitutes interesting, valid, exciting, important sounds, and what are intrusive, invalid, unwanted noises. As such, an account that purported to be a true picture of any actual soundscape would require the full ecology of the field (yet another construction) and such a representation would go well beyond the sensory, incorporating imaginary sounds, undesirable sounds, sounds that are a by-product of desirable events and so on.

There is a direct link to the concept of the soundscape and the practice of a 'sound walk'. On sound walks, participants focus on the sounds that they encounter. These walks are led by an artist or a composer who puts together a walk that seeks out sonic interest points. The most well-known sound walks are those of Max Neuhaus's *LISTEN*, first performed in 1966, for which Neuhaus stamped the wrists of participants with the word 'LISTEN' and they did just that while following him on a walk through urban New York space. Another approach to the sound walk is one where participants listen through headphones to a recording on a personal listening device (mp3 player, smart phone or the like) as they walk through a given location. Artists and composers have used this form to re-experience the everyday environment by telling stories and recounting history. For ease of understanding I will use the term 'audio walk' to reference works that have a recorded audio component and 'sound walks' that have no audio (at least no audio created by the artist).

Audio walks, 'are predicated on an ideology of place as something that is "discoverable" through an instructive, narrated engagement with it' (Moles and Saunders 2015, 154). The act of discovery is conceived of as having a direct connection to the processes of travelling through an environment, the walker learning through a practice of movement. Pointing to the development of audio walks that are more art than information, Kate Moles and Angharad Saunders contend that 'these walks recognize the potential for attunement with the kinaesthetic, synesthetic and sonesthetic perceptions of the walkers, looking to take them to physical and metaphysical places, through memoryscapes and into layered, multiple negotiations of the world around us' (154). This is exactly the point of an ambulatory art practice. The walker comes to the artwork and gains knowledge via the act of physically moving through an architectural space or an environment. Misha Myers states, 'Audio walks create a theatrical auditory space through the sound of voices speaking in the ear. Such works involve the listener-walker-participant as an active performer in the work through a multi-sensory involvement within specific places and landscapes' (2011, 70).

While explicitly pointing to theatre, Myers's discussion here can also be used in thinking through these practices in the contemporary art sphere since, like theatre, the use of these mobile technologies expands the space in which art can happen, and how these works prioritize the 'sensory modes of audience engagement within space' (71). Thus the 'ambulant listener' is guided through space by the artist who engages an active walker via a soundtrack performed somewhat intimately into their ears.

In this context, the work of Janet Cardiff seems tangibly different from most of the works discussed in this book, due simply to its narratival form. Cardiff herself pushes back against any attempt to discuss her work formally in terms of sound alone, and it is difficult to pinpoint moments in interviews where she addresses sound at all. For her, sound is simply the medium by which she tells her stories and seems to be of no particular interest in itself. One of the few actual mentions of sound by the artist occurs in an interview where she states, 'As I said, one of the main things about my work is the physical aspect of sound. A lot of people think it's the narrative quality, but it's much more about how our bodies are affected by sound. That's really the driving force' (Cardiff 2001, 35).

Cardiff's audio walks, which she has made since 1991, involve a complex layering of sound materials. The use of recordings made on the site, of events that happened in the past, combined with the bodily moment through the site, creates a slippage between present sounds and activities and past sounds heard as audio in the recording. The walks are realized for the audience/participant through a combination of an audio recording (played on a portable audio device) and a physical space, most often outdoors. The audience for the work put on headphones and listen to a narrator (Cardiff herself) who instructs them where to go and dictates the timing of their steps (She literally asks the audience to keep in time with the footsteps that can be heard on the audio track.). All the while the narrator points to landmarks or points of interest, warns the audience to avoid certain things, recounts memories and tells stories. There is slippage here between sounds heard in the actual environment, recorded sounds, the story and also a discontinuity between elements of the narration and their existence – or, at times, lack of existence – in the here-and-now of the audience's experience. Adding to the blurred reality of the work is the binaural recording itself. Binaural recording aims to mimic human hearing and uses two microphones that are positioned in the 'ears' of a special mannequin's head or even in or over the ears of an actual person. Thus the microphones record in a similar position to where the ears hear, making for a stereo recording that seems to be three-dimensional, placing sound in relation to actual hearing rather than registering sounds within a more conventional stereo field.

These audio walks could well be thought of as early experiments in augmented reality (AR), as the audience members have a recorded, mediated reality placed over and into non-mediated reality, in much the same way as digitally generated material is merged with the everyday environment in AR works. Thus, knowledge is actually produced in these works through this exchange, with reality bleeding in and out of mediated space. In doing so, audio walks 'negotiate issues of altered perceptions and create an experience of physical immediacy and viscerally through the use of audio and visual material: an experience in which the participants find themselves surrounded by a multilayered, open-ended reality which connects the present with both the past and the future' (Nedelkopoulou 2011, 119).

This sense of an open-ended reality that exists within the audio walk is directed by Cardiff who, according to Derval Tubridy, 'takes us through a specifically delineated location, each step carefully directed by the artist, so that we experience an intimate overlap between the fictional construct of voices and sounds, heard through the headphones worn, and the everyday cacophony of sounds that intrude into the recorded narrative' (2007, 6). As suggested here, what is critical to these works is the overlaying of a fictional sound world with the reality experienced by the audience as they cross the actual road and walk up the actual laneway that is described in the narration. In works such as *Her Long Black Hair* (2004), the ambient sounds recorded on the walk by Cardiff blur with the actual sounds that occur in real time for the participant. They are similar to what is audible to the participant, but the sounds will never be quite the same as those that were recorded. Thus, during the walk, the space of the park itself and the space of the audio work blur, merge and blend such that 'the walker perceives, apprehends, and feels the public space in and through movement. ... The whole trajectory inserts the walker in a movement that enables her or him to experience space in its mixed fictional/physical reality' (Ross 2013, 217).

Discussions of portable listening devices creating a personalized and individuated environment that separates the user from their current location abound – such as Michael Bull's critique of portable music players (2007). Marla Carlson, for her part, repeats the usual expectation that sound technologies distance us from each other and from our present environment, yet in discussing a series of audio walks in New York city after the 9/11 attacks, she points to the way Cardiff employs such technologies 'against its familiar alienating effect' and instead helps 'us to relocate ourselves in the present time and space' (Carlson 2006, 402). Cardiff herself echoes this point when she describes the audio walks:

> Unconsciously the walking pieces are a strange attempt to join our separate worlds through a mediated one, to create a symbiotic relationship between the participant and my voice and body but also to heighten the senses so that you can experience or be part of the environment in which you're walking. Walkmans have always been criticized for creating alienation, but when I first discovered the walking binaural technique I was attracted to the closeness of the sound and the audio bridge between the visual, physical world and my body. To me it was about connection rather than alienation. I think it's partially because the audio on the CD meshes with the audio in the 'real' environment but it's also because sound does come into your unconscious more directly than visual information. (Egoyan 2002, 65)

More recently Cardiff and Miller have begun to make sound and video works in which the audience moves around the walk with a portable media player with a screen. While these works extend many of the same trajectories as the audio walks, the sound-only walks form a more extreme version of the practice in that they do not require visual images of the figures in the story to be created. Christine Ross explains that the screens 'partially fictionalize the walker's view of the space' and that the screen is 'simultaneously a window, a camera, a portable cinema, an archive, and a means of alignment with the artist's initial recording' (2013, 220). For Ross, the technological apparatus – the screen and the headphones – actually 'deepen [the participants'] knowledge of and sensitivity to the space in which they move' (220). Just as the traditional sound walk aims at sensitizing the walker to the sonic actualities of their everyday environment so too, it seems, do the addition of audio and screen to the everyday.

German composer and artist Christina Kubisch also gives her audience what might constitute a deeper knowledge of the everyday environment via her audio walks in which headphones do not play back any pre-recorded audio; instead, they are receivers that are tuned to the electromagnetic hum of the city. Wearing specially constructed headphones, her *Electrical Walks* (2004–) has audiences walk around a city environment with a map that guides them to areas with interesting electromagnetic sounds. The sounds themselves are predominantly those produced by the city's electrical infrastructure – hums with various tics and pops. These sounds change when the headphones are positioned close to screens and mobile phones, and they are also heavily influenced by underground train lines. The feeling when experiencing these works is of dislocation (the sounds are very unlike the sounds we expect to hear, yet they are very clearly associated with the environment and change with the user's interactions with technologies) and connection (a realization that we are surrounded by electromagnetic activity). This new knowledge of our everyday environment creates a sense that our surroundings are filled with unheard electromagnetic radiation.[9]

In this chapter, I have primarily focused on a range of sounds, often noisy and either deliberate or incidental, that can be heard within the walls of the art gallery. These sounds at times enter these spaces as part of the art itself, but as the audience walks into the adjoining gallery, that sound itself swiftly turns into noise as it leaks into the neighbouring gallery and interferes with the contemplation of other discrete artworks. We should also remember that noise enters the gallery through numerous non-art means, from inside as various institutional and non-institutional sound (public announcements and mobile phone rings) and from the outside in the form of everyday sounds of life. What this demonstrates is that the supposedly sacrosanct space of the gallery has never been silent, nor has it ever really approached quietude; instead, we find that galleries are very raucous architectural spaces and that in reality there has been very little real attempt to make them quiet. In the contemporary gallery, quiet is not in fact a desired condition for either art patron or art institution. For better or for worse, patrons want to attend blockbuster exhibitions with the whole family, having a day of entertainment. They enjoy the crowd noises and the part they play in adding to this sound-filled environment. In the case of the art institution, the raised noise floor of the museum signifies the popularity of contemporary exhibition practice and with it the financial value and cultural capital that goes with the attendance figures of large and popular exhibitions and sprawling biennales. Like these unconfinable sounds within the gallery, perhaps discovered through the act of walking, the sounds heard while sound and audio walking outside the bounds of the gallery are constantly mobile in nature and are not perceived as something that requires confinement. After walking and listening outside the gallery and on returning to the art institution, we become fully aware of the discovery of sound through our movement in the art gallery; listening out for the sounds in the adjoining spaces as we walk towards the next room and the next exhibit. In the following section further sound is added to the gallery in the form of music.

3

Musical galleries

As we have already witnessed in this book, 1969 was something of a watershed moment. It was a time when experimentation across the arts was in full swing and the arts were filled for many with the belief that the new way forward was through radical innovation and through the blurring of the old disciplinary boundaries. Key to this belief was the expansion of the art gallery from being merely the context for the exhibit of visual art to an environment in which all forms of the arts could be staged. The art gallery in this moment was reimagined as a place where music, theatre and dance could appear alongside emerging art forms such as performance art and installation.

Music is associated with almost every aspect of the art process. It forms the backdrop to studio practice, commonly played in the artist's studio; music sparks the imagination and is inextricably tied to the creative process. Music is typically played and performed within art museums, whether it is quietly piped into the entranceway to provide a calm backdrop to the various entrance requirements or is set as the soundtrack to the purchase of a catalogue in the museum bookshop. At certain openings a string quartet might be heard playing compositions by Mozart, or perhaps a DJ spins hip-hop. Music regularly takes centre stage in the art space as jazz, Western art music, experimental music, rock and pop are frequently performed in the art museum. The Whitney Museum of American Art holds regular concerts of music, featuring such musicians as The Necks, Takehisa Kosugi, Pauline Oliveros and Cecil Taylor, and MoMA PS1 holds an event entitled Sunday Sessions with DJs, bands and electronic music. On a smaller scale, artist-run galleries house experimental, noise and other extreme musical practices, alongside dance music events and DJ performances. Many artists such as Mike Kelley, Marina Rosenfeld and Christian Marclay also perform music. Artists make music in art school bands, such as Christian Marclay's band Her Bachelors, Even, or in the form of electronic minimalism in the media-rich performances of Royji Ikeda. Music is the content of many artworks, never more so than in video installations such as Pipilotti Rist's *Ever Is Over All* (1997) in which the only sounds are music and the occasional smashing of car windows, or Doug Aitken's *Migration* (2008) with its highly produced atmospheric musical soundtrack. Artists regularly collaborate with musicians on projects, for example Douglas Gordon's collaboration with singer-songwriter Rufus Wainwright for the work *Phantom* (2011), or performance artist Marina Abramović's 2013 collaboration on the music video for Jay Z's 'Picasso Baby', performed in the Pace Gallery in New York. Exhibitions of music can be found in the art museum: for example a collection of Sonic Youth memorabilia was exhibited in the Museum of Contemporary Art, Sydney as part of the exhibition Art/Music: Rock, Pop, Techno (2001). This show also included a concert series held in the nearby Sydney Opera House featuring performances by a number of artists in the exhibition, including Lee Ranaldo, Christian Marclay, Marco Fusinato and Carsten Nicolai.

The use of the gallery for the performance of music is in and of itself an interesting phenomenon; however, this chapter of the book is not simply a history of the art gallery as an alternative concert venue. Instead, the intention of this chapter is to consider these performances as being a part of the art institution and, furthermore, to discuss music in the gallery as more than simply the exploitation of a large open space for music performances. As with previous chapters, this is not intended as a survey or a complete history, nor is it invested in attempting to ascertain who did what first. Instead, 'Musical Galleries' focuses on how the art gallery has shaped the music that is housed within it, how music has shaped the art experience and how music has come to be employed as the content of contemporary art.

'Musical Galleries' aims to re-listen to the evolving role of music within the art gallery. At first, music enters the art space intact, that is, without changing or adapting to the specifics of either the interior architecture or the requirements of the art institution. Focusing on the influential exhibition Anti-Illusion: Procedures/

Materials (19 May to 6 July 1969) held at the Whitney Museum of American Art, and the work of Philip Glass and Steve Reich in the late 1960s, I will argue that music at this time had something to offer the art institution (namely more experimental practices for the voracious art audience to consume) and that the art institution had something to offer the composers (a physical space in which to hold the concerts and an appreciative audience). These two composers' music, in this case, are not directly affected by the art context itself so much as they are given legitimacy by the institution of art, and they took this new validation back to the music world.

Music, however, was directly affected and changed in later art gallery settings. The contextual situation of the gallery and the effects of the art audiences' consumption of music within the exhibition space have generated new approaches to music performance and new musical subgenres. To explore this we will look at two case studies of experimental music series: impermanent.audio and Meeting at Off Site – both of which used small independent galleries to hold their events. Finally, 'Music as Art' will examine recent contemporary art that not only engages music but also produces gallery art for which music becomes both a theme and a medium. This last section will thus register a significant shift in the place of music in relation to art, for in the last decade music has been allowed past the outskirts of art practices and into its museums as bona fide contemporary art. Artists such as Anri Sala and Ragnar Kjartansson have built their careers on art practices for which music *is* art. At this point in history it is then safe to say that the art institution has embraced sound within its exhibition spaces and has begun to implement strategies for its installation, and that this is being spurred on by recent music-driven artworks.

a Anti-Illusion: Steve Reich and Philip Glass

In the first chapter, 'The Empty-sounding Gallery', we saw that a number of works produced in 1969 employed sound (or a lack thereof) to address the experiential qualities of art and music. In that same year, music was a central component to the exhibition Anti-Illusion: Procedures/Materials curated by Marcia Tucker and James Monte. This exhibition stands as a key moment in the development of an art practice that not only expanded beyond modernism and its formalist extension in minimalism, but also introduced an experimental approach to materials and process. Anti-Illusion presented a form of conceptualism where, as the title suggests, practice was based on the combination of procedures and materials. That is, the process of making the work becomes as important as any finished product. The materials explored by the artists extended from the traditional (wood, marble and steel) to the unexplored (flour, music, air, a bank account). The physical artworks were of little consequence and, at the end of the exhibition, the works would have most likely been cleaned away and thrown in the garbage rather than carefully dismantled and packed into shipping crates. Although art in this context is still based on material, these materials are of little or no intrinsic value in and of themselves. As James Monte explained at the time, 'The radical nature of many works in this exhibition depends less on the fact that new materials are being used by the artists than on the fact that the acts of conceiving and placing the pieces take precedence over the object quality of the works' (1969, 4).

Anti-Illusion was based around an understanding of highly contemporary process and materials-based practices, and music was drawn into its ambit. By including composers Philip Glass and Steve Reich, curators Tucker and Monte recognized a procedural similarity between the approach taken to composition by the two musicians and the visual artists included in the exhibition. The years preceding Anti-Illusion had seen the emergence of art practices that incorporated the use of a wide range of materials that would not normally be considered appropriate for serious art, mostly within the field of sculpture. Extending this approach saw the inclusion of not just music but also dance and filmmaking into the exhibition. As will be discussed, the invitation to have their music performed made a lasting impression on Philip Glass and Steve Reich.

Tucker and Monte had only worked at the Whitney for a few months when they conceived the exhibition in January 1969, opening it only months later in May, a quick turnaround by anyone's standards. The curators drew together artists often associated with post-minimalism, such as William Bollinger, Eva Hesse, Robert Morris, Bruce Nauman and Richard Serra. What was striking about the selection was the inclusion of participants not usually associated with art exhibition, namely the composers Glass and Reich, and filmmakers Michael Snow and Robert Fiore, as well as Meredith Monk and James Tenney, who took part in Nauman and Reich's performances, respectively. However, the breadth of artists was not quite as broad as that of the materials used in Anti-Illusion, which included 'flour dust, hay and grease, steel, poured latex, neon and glass, lead, styrofoam blocks, ice and dry leaves, invested money, dog food, rocks, rubberized cheesecloth, and the human body' (Wasserman 1969, 57). For Emily Wasserman, the at times non-visual and impermanent nature of the sculptures reflected the artists' new relationship to these materials: 'The artists' refusal to objectify, to order and to construct permanently or solidly alters the conventional expectations for sculpture as something durable, discreetly formed or built, balanced from part to part, or substantially refined in numerous ways' (57).

These artists were part of a general movement towards dematerialization that emerged, in part, as a reaction to the industrialized, systematic processes of sculptural minimalism, which often resulted in highly polished machine-produced sculptures, such as the work of Donald Judd (Lippard 1973, 5). In the mid-to-late 1960s, influential writer, art critic and curator Lucy Lippard had posited two types of conceptual approach to what she delineated as *dematerialization*, namely art as idea and art as action (Lippard and Chandler 1971, 255). Lippard identifies a number of artists who approach materials not through a structured system but instead allow the materials to determine the form of their work, as 'reflected in the ubiquity of temporary "piles" of materials around 1968' (Lippard 1973, 5). These piles were ephemeral and as such they point to an art practice that is not permanent, timeless and purchasable in the traditional sense. She tells us that the 'premise was soon applied to such ephemeral materials as time itself, space, nonvisual systems, situations, unrecorded experience, unspoken ideas and so on', and subsequently applied to non-physical materials such as 'perception, behavior, and thought processes per se' (5).

In line with this thinking, Marcia Tucker states in the Anti-Illusion catalogue that, 'It has been assumed until recently that sculpture is, by its very nature, three-dimensional, self-contained, and fashioned from relatively durable materials, such as stone, metals, plastics or wood' (1969, 25). Tucker understands that the works do not approach sculpture in the manner she describes above and that, while the outcomes might seem disordered, there is an internal logic, where 'a relational logic has been displaced by a functional one' (27).

The earlier exhibition 9 at Castelli, curated by Robert Morris at Leo Castelli's storage warehouse in December 1968, bears numerous similarities to Anti-Illusion. Many of the artists featured in both shows and the warehouse location clearly had a very direct influence on the curators of Anti-Illusion. The industrial setting for 9 at Castelli is important as the space was nothing like the white-cube galleries, in fact the space only had gallery status provisionally. The exhibition demonstrates a shift from clean white art spaces to an exhibition environment that is directly related to labour through the use of industrial architecture and thereby linking directly to the process-driven practices on display in the exhibition. This move had been underway for some time within artist-run art galleries, but here, a space never intended to be used as an art space, but still owned by a commercial gallery, is used to display the work of its artists. Further, it was situated in Harlem – a neighbourhood rarely frequented by wealthy art buyers – in preference to the actual pristine premises of the commercial gallery situated in a much more affluent part of town.

Bruce Nauman, who was included in 9 at Castelli and Anti-Illusion, installed his first corridor *Performance Corridor* (1969), for Anti-Illusion and he was also included in a series of immaterial process-based performance works that were produced alongside the exhibition in a series of events entitled 'Four Evenings of Extended Time Pieces and a Lecture'. Nauman's duration performance piece was difficult for some, Tucker describes the scene as Nauman, alongside two others, 'bounced backward into a corner for over an hour while a woman in the audience, clearly not part of the piece, moaned audibly, "Please, please stop, please!"' (Tucker and Lou 2008, 84–5)

The piece, entitled *Performance Arena,* was a rare public performance by the artist. Meredith Monk and Judy Nauman, along with Bruce Nauman himself, stood in various corners of the Whitney with their backs to the wall. Over the course of an hour they let themselves fall back on the wall, slapping their hands against it as they did so. After thumping into the wall they bounced back to a standing position and repeated the action. Van Bruggen explains, 'This rigorous, physically exhausting exercise was intensified by the thumping sound it produced' (1988, 236). The performance of *Performance Arena* had various overt sonic outcomes: first, the thwack of the falling bodies reverberated around the art museum's galleries; and, secondly, the rhythms produced by the sound of the falling bodies fell in and out of phase with each other creating a very literal connection to Steve Reich's composition performed the following evening. This phase shifting is crucial to the work in that the performers did not at all attempt to stay in time but could not help falling in and out of time with each other. Nauman's work, as has been discussed numerous times in this book, draws together several strands of practice that are under investigation from 1969, a year that increasingly seems pivotal in the development of gallery sound. In this case, the performance sits between the practices of performance art, dance and music and can also be understood as drawing on his film and video recordings of his private studio performances. The piece is also influenced by the compositions of Reich that used phase shifting and, as we shall see, Nauman himself took part in Reich's performance for Anti-Illusion.

In attendance at *Performance Arena* was Dan Graham who wrote about the work and also Reich's composition the following evening. Graham was meticulous in his detailed description, comparing the difference in the sound produced by the falling body of Nauman to that of Monk: 'The impact of Nauman's fall was sharp and thudding, causing considerable reverberation in the structure of the building (expressed as sound), while Monk, dressed in black tights, hit much more softly and without either the periodic intensity or exactitude in timing of Nauman – some of her "hits" even having a discernibly different tone' (1993, 48). With the same intensity of focus as the performance work, Graham recorded his experience of Steve Reich's *Pendulum Music* (1968) (45–6). He discusses the disparity in timing between the pendulum swing of the microphones across the speakers and the regimented timing of a metronome.

Reich premiered *Pendulum Music* on 27 May 1969, for the final event for 'Four Evenings of Extended Time Pieces and a Lecture'. In an often-reproduced photograph taken moments before the action begins, we see the four performers: Bruce Nauman, Michael Snow, Richard Serra and James Tenney. Each is holding a microphone attached by a long cable to the top of a microphone stand. There is a fifth figure, Reich himself, who stands over a table crammed with electronics that were, for the most part, used in the performance of the other compositions.

The four holding the microphones aloft are about to let them go and, by doing so, set in motion the performance of the work. This in effect is the only deliberate action in this performance and what follows is pure process. Once dropped, the microphone swings across a speaker that is placed facing up, producing a 'whoop' (in Reich's words) as they pass by. The sound is pure feedback created by the microphone being too close to its own sounding through the speaker. At the time Alan Kriegsran described *Pendulum Music's* resultant feedback as generating 'a giddy blare of whistles, wows and undulations, all varying in accordance with the decaying swing of the mikes' (1969, 7). The bursts of feedback become longer as the swinging microphones lose momentum and slow down and, in addition, since this can never happen in a uniform manner across four different set-ups, the four systems fall in and out of phase with each other. When they cease to move, they create a continuous state of feedback, signalling that the performance is over. Reich describes the work as 'the ultimate process piece. It's me making my peace with Cage. It's audible sculpture. If it's done right, it's kind of funny' (2000).

This pure process piece was discovered by accident while Reich was on a trip to Boulder, Colorado to collaborate on an avant-garde theatre event. Reich was in a studio with Nauman and William T. Wiley, an associate and collaborator from Reich's time in the San Francisco Bay Area and Nauman's professor from UC Davis. Reich describes his discovery:

> I had one of these Wollensak tape recorders. ... I [was] holding the microphone, which was plugged into the back of the machine so it could record. The speaker was turned up. Being out West, I let it swing back and forth like a lasso. As it passed by the speaker of the machine it went 'whoop!' and then it went away. We were all laughing at this and the idea popped into my mind that if you had two or three of these machines, you would have this audible sculpture phase piece. (Cole 2014, 234)

In an interview for *Artforum*, Michael Nyman describes *Pendulum Music* as the most impersonal, emblematic and didactic process work, while also being sculptural. Reich regarded the physical placement of the equipment as integral to the work: 'In many ways, you could describe *Pendulum Music* as audible sculpture, with the objects being the swinging microphones and the loudspeakers. I always set them up quite clearly as sculpture. It was very important that the speakers be laid flat on the floor, which is obviously not usual in concerts' (Nyman 1976, 305).

While clearly a musical composition, *Pendulum Music* draws on sculptural tools and also temporal methods that are not traditionally Western music-based. Marcia Tucker connects Steve Reich and Philip Glass with the new approaches to sculpture displayed in Anti-Illusion through their use of time pointing out that in their work,

> actual time is a crucial factor in their music; it offers no illusion of temporality other than that which exists in the performance of their pieces. They have no beginning, middle or end – only a sense of an isolated present. This present exists because of a deliberate and unrelenting use of repetition which destroys the illusion of musical time and focuses attention instead on the material of the sounds and on their performance. (Tucker 1969, 36)

In his doctoral dissertation on the Philip Glass Ensemble between 1966 and 1976, David Chapman too is drawn to time within the compositions of both Reich and Glass at this time. Chapman describes, 'The listener's attention, freed from concerns about virtual or implicit musical time, turns to other matters, namely the tangible materiality of the musical sound and the bounded realities of the performance' (2013, 76).

In addition to the thematic connection to the exhibition, both composers had close ties to the visual art scene of the mid-to-late 1960s. In the early years of Glass's and Reich's careers, the most likely place to experience a performance of their compositions was within an art gallery. There is a very simple reason for this, but the outcomes and influences of these performances are much more telling. The simple reason, from the perspective of Glass and Reich, was that they could not get their work performed in concert halls. It does not get much simpler than that. What is not so clear is why major art galleries and the art museums (including the Whitney, Guggenheim and the MoMA) welcomed these musical performances within their hallowed art spaces.

At the time several reviewers noted that art galleries were being used for the performance of Glass's and Reich's compositions. John Rockwell explained, 'The music is new and not likely to be heard in conventional concert halls. One can more often encounter it in lofts, or Greenwich Village galleries, or museums uptown. … Amplification is screwed up to the point of pain' (2013, 48).

In the same review he further expresses this insight: 'Artists, unlike musicians, have embraced Mr. Glass's and Mr. Reich's works from the first, not least because of the obvious esthetic similarities between this music and recent New York art' (48).

Chapman argues that the audiences most open to Glass's performances in the late 1960s and early 1970s were the Manhattan Downtown visual art and performance audiences – to the point of an implicit social contract between the composer and those audiences (2013, 99–100). Ross Cole, who has written about Reich's career in the late 1960s, makes a similar observation about Reich: 'The existence of such connections [to the visual arts] underscores the necessity of situating Reich's early work away from musical institutions in order to understand how it made sense to listeners and why he came to adopt shifting aesthetic alignments. This perspective calls for a more nuanced view of minimal art and its relationship to music' (Cole 2014, 218).

Cole describes Reich's arrival back in New York from San Francisco in 1965 where he found himself in between the scenes that had and were developing at that time. Reich did not fit into the previous generation's approach to music (Cage, Brown, Feldman, Wolff), nor did he have connections to the longer form drone approach of La Monte Young and his circle (217). Reich was, however, closely associated with various visual arts scenes at this time and, because of the support they showed him, he gravitated towards such scenes and soon employed their art spaces as performance venues.

A similar experience arose for Glass: unable to have his work performed and working by day as a plumber, Glass was drawn into the visual art scene. This included a close relationship with Richard Serra for whom Glass was a studio assistant and sometimes collaborator. Serra states:

> I had a private need to keep my creative insistence open and found sympathy and encouragement from other artists in

> the same straits [referring to being outside of the sanctioned institutions of their practice], namely Bob Smithson, Eva Hesse, Bruce Nauman, Michael Heizer, Phil Glass, Joan Jonas, Michael Snow. What was interesting about this group of people was that we did not have any shared stylistic premises, but what was also true was that everybody was investigating the logic of material and its potential for personal extension – be it sound, lead, film, body, whatever. (Serra and Weyergraf 1980, 136)

It can be said that the art world has, since the late modernist period, been open to highly experimental practices. As can be seen in the cases of Reich and Glass, this extends to practices outside of visual art. If the most prestigious space for the display of the visual arts is the art museum, the equivalent in the world of music is surely the grand concert hall. Reich and Glass performed their compositions in all of the major New York art museums and, by all accounts, these performances drew large audiences and positive receptions. Thus it is certainly not the case that these composers only received underground attention within the visual arts, as they drew recognition from its major institutions. This level of support and openness can be understood as part of the art world's strategy to draw everything inside its remit. The adage that anything and everything can be art is taken at its word by the institution of art. In this case, however, the compositions of Reich and Glass remain music, as one would never confuse these musical performances with visual art. Perhaps this opens an interesting can of worms, as in the case of Reich we have a composer who writes a piece of process music and has it performed in a manner that might be likened to performance art, using a staging that is described by him as sculptural, within an art museum, and yet it resists attempts to turn it into visual art. It resists even a blurring of the disciplinary boundary perhaps because Glass and Reich are so fervently set within the institution of music and have remained so for their entire careers. Furthermore, as Cole attests, 'The conventions of New York's downtown artworld enabled Reich's phase shifting compositions to be recognized and validated (albeit reluctantly at times) *as* music' (2014, 240). By performing music within the art gallery, Glass and Reich had their compositions validated within Western art music at a time when official institutions were unprepared to do so.

The discussion around the audience reaction to the performances is also very different from that of the later concerts, in particular those of Reich. Reviews do not mention the audience being dissatisfied, booing, yelling or of applauding to hasten the end of a performance.[1] Instead, we read that the audience sprawls out on pillows or sits transfixed. The audiences for these performances are in attendance to have new experiences and may well not be people who would normally attend concerts in concert halls. The gallery as a venue draws in an audience who are not only receptive to experimentation but thrive on it. Whole programmes of new music by Reich and Glass are programmed for the art spaces, an event that is markedly different from the regular music concert where numerous composers are featured, most of whom are long deceased. In the latter setting the new work is at best barely tolerated and at worst hated by an audience there to hear their favourite works by Beethoven or Mozart.

Architecturally, the concert hall is designed for the aural and visual contemplation of music. This is made apparent by the seating configuration of most concert halls. Seats are upright and fixed, the audience expected to remain seated for the duration of the performance. The seats themselves face the stage and the audience's attention is focused on the performer in front of them. In short, the concert hall is designed to foster a specific listening experience.[2] The architecture of the gallery bears little if any resemblance to a concert hall, possessing no permanent stage and no predetermined placing of seating. As such, there is an almost unlimited number of possible permutations for the configuration of the space in which a performance takes place and the disposition of the audience in relation to that space. These freedoms allow for the production of events that rethink the proscenium arch and this in turn enables the audience to listen to this music in 'new' ways (for Western art music at least). In other forms of music this freedom of audience listening modes was far from new in the late 1960s. That being said, these modes of listening were not available in the concert hall setting and thus allowed for a new freedom and a new audience for the music. Carman Moore noted this casual listening environment in a review of Reich's tape music at Park Place.[3] She describes a 'new listening style for electronic music audiences … foam-rubber pillows were made available for sitting or sprawling' (Moore 1966, 8). Alan Kriegsman notes that the audience for Reich's performance at the Whitney consisted of 'young people in hip attire, [who] sat transfixed on the gallery floor like a circle of communing Druids' (1969, 7).

The freedom to stage the performances beyond the proscenium arch was capitalized upon in Glass's performance at Anti-Illusion. The performance was the premiere of the newly formed Philip Glass Ensemble, which performed from the centre of the gallery, as it would famously continue to do. Set up in the middle of the gallery, the ensemble was surrounded by the audience with speakers placed in the corners of the gallery facing towards the musicians. This configuration places the musicians in the 'sweet spot' of audio projection for a quadraphonic set-up. The audience is free to sit anywhere in the gallery to witness the performance (Chapman 2013, 78).

After this phase of emerging practice, which ended in the early 1970s, both composers returned to the concert hall as the primary venue for the performance of their music. These early gallery concerts set up their careers and created a large and appreciative audience for their music, overcoming the initial difficulties the composers encountered in persuading a more traditionally orientated music audience of the value of their minimal compositions. For the art museums, they had set a precedent that opened the exhibition spaces to high-profile performances and gave evidence as to the high level of interest in experimental music from their patrons. Art galleries have continued to provide space for music performances across most musical genres and furthermore, rather than simply providing a space for performance, the architecture and the culture of exhibition spaces have influenced how we listen to this music and how the music itself has been generated.

b Off Site and impermanent.audio: experimental and improvised

Galleries provide a container for music and that containment itself can influence the music produced within it. As discussed earlier in *Gallery Sound*, the white-cube gallery is far from a neutral space and in terms of sound it can be highly problematic. One effect of the space in terms of the performance of music is that the hard, flat and square walls allow sound to reflect around the architecture, producing strong reverberation and long decay times. With a relatively simple sound, such as a clap, the sound reflects off the walls and bounces around. If instead of a clap we produce a sound with a longer duration, such as an electronic sound or a sequence of electronic sounds, which is to say a sound that lasts for longer than an instant, the overlapping reverberations of sound in space create numerous additive effects. When these are undesired, the gallery structure can cause a clean electronic sound to become muddy as it folds over itself, sounding for much longer than perhaps wanted. These reverberations can also be the desired effect, creating the effects sought within the composition, such as for Alvin Lucier's *I am Sitting in a Room*. Lucier's piece could not have been made without these acoustic properties, but the gallery space can adversely affect sounds and force the performer to modify their expectations or even modify the sounds they use so as to utilize or work with the reflective space rather than rail against it. This, it will be argued, has generated new ways of performing and of listening to music.

In the previous examples of Glass and Reich, they simply performed their music in the gallery as it was originally composed, but in the examples that will be discussed below it is not always possible to simply play works as they were originally intended in the art gallery. In addition to the architecture that physically affects the sound within the gallery, the technical limitations and the culture of the gallery also influence the outcome of performances held within it. It would be difficult, for example, to stage a rock concert with a full backline of guitar amplifiers in an art gallery, mostly due to the possibility of a deafening volume of sound that would emanate from such a set-up (although not impossible, as has been discussed in relation to Fusinato's gallery performances). As well as the limitations of volume within the gallery space, performance is also constrained by the surrounds of the gallery, including neighbouring business and residential housing. Sound in the gallery is already difficult to contain but in addition, many forms of music actually seek volume as a crucial element of their performance and this is often the cause of noise complaints from local residences. Performers of music who especially utilize small independent galleries have developed new modes of performance to address the challenges posed by both the gallery space and its surrounding environment.

Between 2000 and 2006 I produced a monthly event, impermanent.audio.[4] In its initial year it was housed at Imperial Slacks, an artist-run gallery located within a light industrial building in central Sydney. The gallery was on the third floor and there were no issues with neighbours and noise, allowing for the possibility of high-volume performances. Yet the event developed a reputation for intensely focused listening to often extremely quiet electronic experimental music. The reason for the intensity and low volume were twofold: the gallery environment and the specificity of amplification.

impermanent.audio was afforded the freedom to lay out the gallery in any way required for each event. As discussed in the previous section, art spaces do not generally have a stage or even a front as such; thus the room can be set up as desired and in a manner that best suits the particularities of a given event. The most elaborate staging at impermanent.audio within Imperial Slacks occurred for a performance by the Spanish musician Francisco López in 2001. López's live performances are designed for both a spatialized and close-up listening experience. On entering the performance space, the audience becomes aware of an array of speakers installed around the perimeter of the gallery and a mixing desk at the centre (accompanied by, in this case, three CD players). One of the defining elements of a López performance is his requirement that the audience all wear blindfolds for the duration of the work. He believes that by removing sight as a sense the audience is able to concentrate more closely on the audio and experience a much deeper engagement with the spatialized sounds (López 2004). This is quite simply because they are not watching López perform, nor are they distracted by watching other people present. As well as blindfolding the audience, López rejects a normative concert set-up that would place the musician in front of the audience, believing that it imparts a visual listening method, as line of sight is the overarching conception of the stage space. This he believes is contrary to the manner in which we actually listen:

> As opposed to the directionality of visual elements, sound is perceived coming from every direction. ... Sound perception is simultaneously multi-directional. In a live event this allows immersion, intensified phenomenological experience, to 'be inside' the sound instead of listening to it, achievable by very

> simple and widely available technical means: An array of speakers around the audience controlled from the center of the space. (2004)

With the performer in the centre of the space, the audience is required to sit or lie on the floor around the performer (if no seating is available), in a manner similar to what was witnessed at the early performances of Reich in art galleries. My experience of the performance was one of deep engagement. Freed from the necessities of the proscenium arch, López can think about the room as a whole which is organized not to enable the audience to witness the spectacle of music but, rather, to be immersed in the experience of sound.

impermanent.audio was notorious for drawing in an engaged and highly attentive audience. The series was curated to deliver to the expectations of an art audience seeking a new experience and thus ready to engage in silent and focused listening, rather than those of a popular music audience concerned not only with the music but also with the social aspects of concert-going. While quiet audiences who do not speak throughout performances may be commonplace in many music scenes, it certainly was not the case in Sydney for experimental music gigs at this time. Many of the events occurring in Sydney in the late 1990s were staged in one-off spaces, such as warehouses, pubs, bars and social clubs. These performances were infamous for their noisy and inattentive audiences. For the impermanent.audio series I focused the audiences' attention by using triggers for silence including changing the lighting state, closing the bar for the duration of the performance, introducing the musicians before they played and, finally and most scandalously, asking disruptive audience members to leave – and while this was only necessary a few times, it was a highly effective method for schooling the audience who came to the shows. The audience for this monthly event thus arrived expecting to listen closely and quietly, prepared to sit for upward of thirty minutes on the hard gallery floor without feeling the need to converse with those around them. This silence reached a palpable quietude in which the quietest of performances could be played. At one such event I noted that during the long gaps between sounds performed by Toshimaru Nakamura I could hear no noises coming from the audience at all – no coughing, sniffing, shuffling in chairs, no movement at all.

Alongside the staging and attentive audience there was another factor that brought about the creation of the culture and scene around impermanent.audio, namely the amplification employed. impermanent.audio began as a very small underground event that was completely funded from door charges. Due to the lack of funds, a small PA was borrowed from an artist who resided in the venue. The PA had a tendency to blow a fuse when low frequencies were run through it at volume and, as a result, performers were required to play more quietly than they normally would. These quietened performances forced the musicians to think about the role of volume within their live practice and to adjust for the specificities of the PA. This was only possible as the audience for the events was prepared to listen in silence and expected this kind of listening experience. This quiet and attentive audience therefore allowed musicians to experiment with very low-volume performances and this often had unexpected aural outcomes. For example, during a performance by the Sydney group Stasis Duo, the very low-volume feedback and sine tones framed other sounds occurring in the environment, such as the whine of a nearby lift shaft, and also caused aural hallucinations, with some audience members believing they were hearing voices when no one was speaking.

Closely associated with impermanent.audio was the series Meeting at Off Site run by Tetuzi Akiyama, Toshimaru Nakamura and Taku Sugimoto. The series was first held in August 2000 and ran until January 2003 in the small Off Site gallery in Yoyogi, Tokyo. The gallery itself was very small and situated in a converted residential house. The main gallery space was downstairs where the performances occurred, and upstairs contained a bar, a small record store and bookshop. Off Site became known as the centre of a small movement of Japanese musicians who improvised with their instruments in a fashion that produced very small sounds, which if they were amplified, were done so at very low volume. Musicians working with more traditional instruments, such as guitars, might play very few notes, as did Taku Sugimoto, or extend and expand the way they played their guitar like Tetuzi Akiyama. The improvisers working with electronics did something far more extreme, however, and emptied their electronic tools of content in order to play the tool itself. In the case of Sachiko M this meant emptying her sampler of all samples and playing the inbuilt test tone, which was a simple sine wave. Toshimaru Nakamura for his part performed a 'no-input mixing board'. The concept is, of course, somewhat oxymoronic, since a mixing board is generally used to control and equalize inputs from various devices such as record players, MP3 players, electronic instruments or live recorded sound. Nakamura, however, instead set up a feedback system where he connected the inputs to the outputs, creating a feedback loop that he played in performance.

This small scene was also known for performing at very low volume, at times on the very threshold of audibility. There was a contextual reason for this, as residential houses surrounded the gallery and the walls between the buildings were very thin. As such the neighbours could hear the music, so the gallery required performances to be held at low volume. Minoru Hatanaka explains, 'This is why it is inevitable that the music performed at Off Site be so quiet as to require listeners to prick up their ears to hear it. … Careful not to make a sound, the listeners remain so still and listen so attentively that they can hear the breathing of the people next to them' (2002–3, 9). I can confirm that on the occasions I attended concerts at Off Site I could actually hear the breathing of the audience member sitting next to me. So quiet was the gallery that musicians actually performed on their electronic instruments without using amplification. In August 2002, Otomo Yoshihide and Tetuzi Akiyama performed on turntables without plugging them into a sound system, instead making acoustic sounds with various objects and the rotating platter (Kelly 2009, 194). In February 2003, according to Nakamura, Australian artist Matthew Earle performed on a sampler that was not plugged in, the only sounds heard therefore being the clicking of the buttons being pressed by the musician.

While the examples of impermanent.audio and Meeting at Off Site might be extreme, they aim to illustrate that the gallery context, including its infrastructure, actually produced new ways of performing and creating music. Small galleries are commonly employed as makeshift venues for music and in the process of using them they exert an influence on some of the practices of the music being performed within them. This has not remained a one-way influence. I want to argue that music itself has not only been embraced by the institution of art as an entity separate to art, but that in the last decade music has actually become a medium and theme within international contemporary art. It may be that for this to occur the art institution had to come to terms with the breadth of sounds that are found within the gallery and that this has happened to such a level that music has been embraced by art within its bounds.

c Music as art

Music has been performed in the art gallery under numerous guises, but in the last decade contemporary art has only just begun to integrate music into its remit, becoming a theme for a number of contemporary artists. Artists like Janet Cardiff (Canada), Marco Fusinato (Australia), Ragnar Kjartansson (Iceland), Angelica Mesiti (Australia), Ari Benjamin Meyers (USA), Marina Rosenfeld (USA) and Anri Sala (Albania) have integrated music into their practice. In many instances, and perhaps as a result of the evolving art entertainment industry, the music they use is as likely to be popular music as the kind of experimental music or abstract sound that might seem to have a more natural connection to the art world. This is not to say, however, that the use of music in art is something that has never been heard before, but here there is an intensified engagement with music as the dominant element or medium within the art, that is, music is the artwork.

The installations by many of the above-mentioned artists feature projections alongside which sit not the small speakers usually found in contemporary galleries but, rather, full-sized sound systems, with speakers and amplification designed to fill spaces considerably larger than the galleries in which they are found. The use of the PA within the gallery may well have reached its zenith when Marco Fusinato employed a line array for *Aetheric Plexus*. However, while Fusinato's work directly critiques the arts entertainment industry and thus took the use of the sound system far beyond what was necessary for such a space, other artists such as Anri Sala make use of sound systems to integrate audio of a far higher quality than would generally be possible in an art gallery setting into their installation, thereby according a particular privilege and importance to sound as an element of equal, if not greater, importance to the overall experience of the piece as its visual elements.

The fact that music has been so thoroughly integrated into artists' practices and shown in major art museums and international biennales demonstrates the willingness of the art world to take on music and the intensification of sound within the art space. This has occurred at a time when understandings of sound within the gallery have reached a level of maturity that has allowed for this to happen. Art galleries have, perhaps, until recently struggled to develop a strategy for the installation of sound and are conventionally more likely to invest in high-definition video projectors than good-quality sound systems. It is not uncommon to see projectors that cost many thousands of dollars mounted on museum ceilings, while small cheap black or white speaker boxes are affixed to the wall or ceiling of the gallery. In 2005–6 I noticed that Sydney's artist-run spaces commonly owned at least one projector but often had little more than a home stereo system for sound. These small sound systems had trouble providing a fullness to sound in the gallery space. At the time I believed this was one of the main reasons why the local art schools were producing graduates adept at video production but with little idea of how to produce sound. Why would a student invest time working on developing their sound practice when the audio track to their work was most likely only going to be amplified through a low-quality sound system? Much better to spend your time on the projection.

Another common issue with speakers in the gallery is one of placement. To maintain the visual continuity of the exhibition environment the technologies of audiovisual presentation are most often hidden from sight. This is not so problematic for the visual side of mediatized art as the frame of the flat screen monitor closely resembles the frame of a painting and a video projector can be removed from sight by installing it in the ceiling. Speakers are not quite so easily handled as they break up the clean projection-filled wall and as such are often relegated to the ceiling or are placed behind the viewer (a problematic tactic as we watch the screen in front of us while hearing sound emanating from speakers behind us). Brent Grayburn's *Flicker* (2007), installed at Artspace, Sydney, is a case in point. The work had a highly produced sound track composed by music producer Scott Horscroft that relied on surround sound, yet strangely the speakers were placed high in the ceiling and angled down towards the audience, removing the desired sense of spatiality. The poorly installed speaker is a common occurrence within gallery spaces, where visuality is preferenced over aurality.

However, for the recent wave of artists working with music, this is not an issue. Many of them celebrate the speaker as a critical and visible component of their installations. The lower floor of the survey show Anri Sala: Answer Me, at the New Museum in New York (2016), is a case in point. This section of the exhibition featured the works *The Present Moment (in B-flat)* (2014) and *The Present Moment (in D)* (2014). Sala regularly produces pairs of works that are very closely related and designed to be exhibited together; in this case two versions of the same Arnold Schoenberg composition *Verklärte Nacht* (1899). The installation of the work for Anri Sala: Answer Me consisted of a two-channel HD projection with a twenty-channel sound installation. Twenty large black speakers hung from the gallery ceiling throughout the space, surrounding the lift shaft in the centre of the space. While other works were present on this floor, they all resonated to the soundtrack of *The Present Moment.* Not only is the sound purposely uncontained, filling the entire exhibition space both with the audio and the very physically present speakers, but when attending to the other works exhibited in the gallery, that experience was always accompanied by the sound of *The Present Moment.* Sala draws attention to the speakers filling the spaces with music and allowing the speakers to be a predominant aspect of the exhibition as a whole; the speakers are the aural and visual focus of the installations.

Sala describes the role of music within his installations, stating:

> Even if I'm a visual artist, I build on the sound, I build with sound and in the process I let sound trigger its visual reality. The challenge is how to make this process visible, without letting images diminish the sound. And this creates a different kind of film, where music never operates as mere film music, but is the product of an act as opposed to an illustration of an action. (2013)

This challenge, as outlined by Sala, is present throughout his work and could palpably be felt over the three floors of installations for his survey show at the New Museum. The other two floors are equally driven by the logic of Sala's speaker installation. There are numerous large-scale projections, but what is most notable is the abundance of PA speakers throughout the exhibition. The cavernous galleries are filled with music and, interestingly, each space is treated differently in terms of acoustic dampening. On one floor, alternating works are projected on both sides of a large screen that hangs in the centre of the gallery, with large black speakers dangling from the ceiling. This gallery has no acoustic dampening and the sounds, which at times include a live saxophone performance, are extremely animated and reverberant in the space.

Answer me (2008), one of the works screened in this gallery, focuses on a drummer who is filmed close-up and from behind, alternating with a woman demanding of the drummer that he 'answer me'. The work is set in a building constructed on top of an artificial hill in the almost completely flat city of Berlin:

> At the height of the Cold War, since this was one of the tallest spots in Berlin, the NSA decided to build an eavesdropping centre on top of the hill: an observatory with radars cloaked in a series of elevated domes, after Buckminster Fuller's design. ... The moment you entered, it felt like you were going inside a huge cathedral with a geodesic dome. (Sala and Gioni 2016, 88)

The drummer plays within one of the domes and the sound of his drums reverberates around the otherwise empty space. As with Nauman's *Six Sound Problems*, we hear the overlapping of reverberations, as the space in which the drummer performs is played into the reverberant space of the art gallery. Sala's focus for the work was the reverberant character of the room. He explains, 'I wondered how awkward silences would sound in a place of extreme loudness, under the influence of the overwhelming echo of a geodesic dome' (88).

At the other extreme in terms of room acoustics is the installation of the pair of works *Ravel Ravel* (2013) and *Unravel* (2013) on the top floor of the museum. These artworks are formed around two separate performances of Maurice Ravel's *Piano Concerto in D for the Left Hand* (1930), composed to be performed with the left hand only. The virtuosic pianists Louis Lortie and Jean-Efflam Bavouzet were filmed separately, and as their performances are ever so slightly different, this causes the duo to slide in and out of sync as the work progresses. The installation is in a very large room treated with acoustic wedges that cover the walls and the ceiling. The wedges are the same as those used in an anechoic chamber and

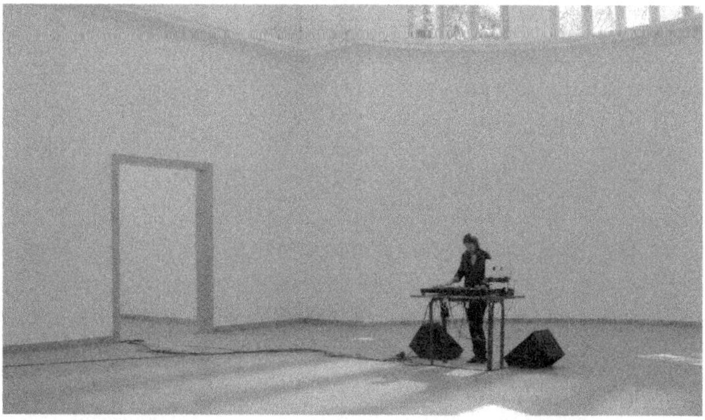

FIGURE 9 Anri Sala, *Unravel* (2013). Courtesy of Galerie Chantal Crousel, Paris; Marian Goodman Gallery; Hauser & Wirth; kurimanzutto, Mexico City.

create a non-reverberant space into which sound is projected. Many speakers fill this gallery, creating an immersive environment, but, peculiarly, the effect of the wedges is negligible simply because there are so many speakers producing so much sound in the space that it is not possible to experience any anechoic chamber-like effects. In the adjoining room the work *Unravel* (2013) focuses on the hands and facial expression of a DJ who plays two records, one from each rendition of the concerto: 'In *Unravel,* Chloe – a DJ and music producer – attempts to untangle what has been entangled in *Ravel Ravel.* She tries to revoke the distinctions between the two performances of the pianists Bavouzet and Lortie by cancelling the interval between their respective performances' (96).

The performance involves the DJ's attempt to sync the two performances across her two turntables, failure written across her face as her attempts are thwarted by the often minute differences between the two recordings.

Sala's artwork, with its focus on music, testifies to the inclusion of music in contemporary art and it also demonstrates that the art institution is capable of understanding and supporting artwork for which sound is the primary motivation of a major survey exhibition. Serious investment, both aesthetic and financial, has been directed towards the sound within this exhibition and the pay-off is three floors of intensified audio experiences. With Anri Sala: Answer Me, the need to draw attention to a special category of art entitled 'sound art' is discarded; instead, what we have is a well-managed and mature engagement with sound, within the framework of contemporary art.

Sala has worked closely with collaborators who contribute to the compositional elements of these works. One of these collaborators, Berlin-based American artist Ari Benjamin Meyers, has a background as a composer of new music. Meyers began to move into contemporary art in 2007 while working as the musical director for Il Tempo Del Postino (2007) curated by Hans Ulrich Obrist and Philippe Parreno. Il Tempo Del Postino was a stage musical commissioned by the Manchester International Festival and included work by well-known artists such as Tacita Dean, Doug Aitken, Douglas Gordon, Olafur Eliasson, Rirkrit Tiravanija and Anri Sala. The event employed music as its primary focus, requiring the contemporary artists to develop music-driven artworks. Meyers's role was that of a traditional musical director, working closely with the artists to create the music for the event and by the association with these artists Meyers gained entrance to the art institution.

Meyers had felt restricted by his background as a composer who wrote scores for the concert hall, coming to the conclusion that the institution of music gave little room for the critique of the structure or the environment for concerts, which was in stark contrast to the highly critical approach in the production of much contemporary art: 'Even when the music itself is very contemporary, the whole situation around it is still very, very conservative. So, even in the case of contemporary music, essentially you're either giving concerts or you're making records – and that's about it' (Meyers 2013).

New music compositions are most often premiered as one small part of a larger concert in which well-known compositions are the main feature and the key reason the audience is in attendance, and as such the new piece is in general tolerated rather than loved. Given that a group of highly trained musicians is required to perform the piece, as well as access to a concert hall to play in, it is as a result not uncommon for the premiere of such a piece to be its only performance. Some of the key differences between the concert hall and the gallery – differences that are of particular interest to Meyers – are rooted in the manner in which audience members approach works within the respective environments and the freedoms the art gallery allows for the presentation of his work. Where a concert is bounded by a precise timeframe (e.g. 7:00 to 9:00 pm on Saturday night), an exhibition is open across a number of weeks and gallery opening hours extend much longer than a regular concert duration. Audiences can attend an exhibition at whatever time suits them during opening hours and they are free to come and go as they wish – all attributes of an exhibition not usually extended to a concert. Within this frame Meyers has produced works that utilize the opportunity for extended durations that are not afforded by the concert hall. For example, his exhibition Black Thoughts (2013) included the composition *Serious Immobilities* for which three musicians (singer, bass and electric guitar) performed the piece for the duration of the gallery's opening hours. The gallery itself was empty but for the instruments and any gallery patrons in attendance. The performance continued throughout the day in the white-walled and black-carpeted space whether or not any gallery visitors were present. Much like La Monte Young's *Dream House*, visitors arrived to a work in progress and they were free to sit with the music, amble around the space and leave whenever they were ready.

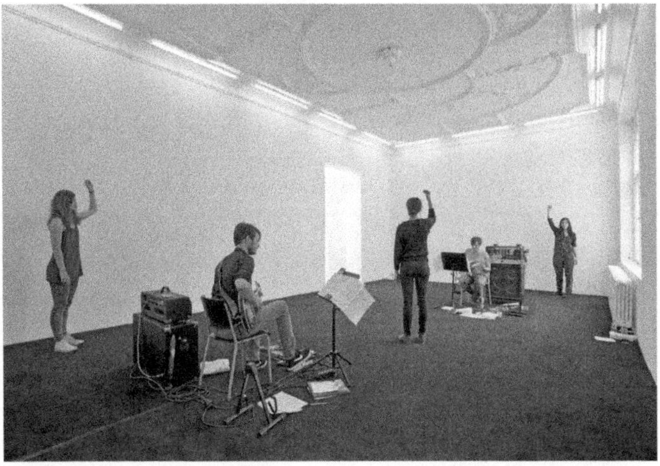

FIGURE 10 Ari Benjamin Meyers, *Serious Immobilities* (2013), exhibition view (detail). Courtesy of the artist and Esther Schipper, Berlin. Photograph by Andreas Rossetti.

These freedoms are of course not allowed within the concert hall. Patrons are expected to remain seated for the full course of the performance and leaving is generally understood as an explicit protest directed at the performance underway. A concert is bounded not only by the duration of the performance but also by the financial costs of staging it. The overheads of such an event are extremely high and thus a certain number of patrons are required to purchase tickets, often at a premium, and the duration of the event has a budgetary impact as many employees are paid by the hour. Meyers's work *Solo* (2009) takes full advantage of the possibilities of a small audience by allowing only one visitor at a time into a tiny four square metre gallery. Those who attended this exhibition entered the gallery where they experienced a six-minute live performance in the most intimate of settings.

The question of just how music is accepted as contemporary art in these cases can be posed to Meyers, and it is a question to which he has provided an answer, saying, 'What does it mean to exhibit music? ... It's just a medium – a time-based medium like film, video, or performance' (Meyers 2013). Herein lies the key, we already understand that anything and everything can be art (via Duchamp), and if film, video and performance can be art, and this is readily accepted, then surely music can be too.

Similar to Meyers, music is a central component of the work of New York artist and musician Marina Rosenfeld, except that she has a background in fine art rather than classical music. Her orchestrated performance pieces employ mostly untrained or young people to play live music within the art gallery, alongside prerecorded electronic music, field recordings and physical objects. Rosenfeld's longest running project is her *Sheer Frost Orchestra*, which she began in 1993 while an art student at the California Institute of the Arts. While the orchestra constantly changes its membership, it is formed for each performance from seventeen female participants who are invited by Rosenfeld to perform electric guitar with bottles of nail polish. Many of these guitarists are untrained, learning the required extended techniques from the artist in the lead up to the performance. For her, 'The point is to recruit non-musicians and enable them to transform themselves into musicians or, as I sometimes characterize it, people "making musical decisions in real time"' (Rosenfeld 2002, 59).

In performance a colourful array of guitars are lined up on the floor where they are played by women sitting or kneeling in front of them with the guitar sounds being amplified through a row of small black guitar amps behind them. The ensemble performs using extended techniques to play their guitars, sliding and hammering the guitar strings with nail polish bottles, and thereby eliciting an array of sliding tones and improvised juxtapositions of tone clusters. The orchestra has only performed in art galleries, including the Whitney and the Tate Modern, and while the work could be understood as music that is performed within the bounds of the gallery (like any music concert performed within the art institution), in this case the context of the art museum allows for it to be read conceptually, in a manner that it perhaps could not be if performed in a live music venue. Seth Kim-Cohen points to Rosenfeld's interrogation of 'the conditions of musical production and reception, of music's symbolic and social space' (Kim-Cohen 2009, 248). This is manifested through the social and relational situation of the workshop, the performance itself and the further social situations that occur after the performance. While the work can and should be listened to as music, it also elicits a critical reading that looks to the social and

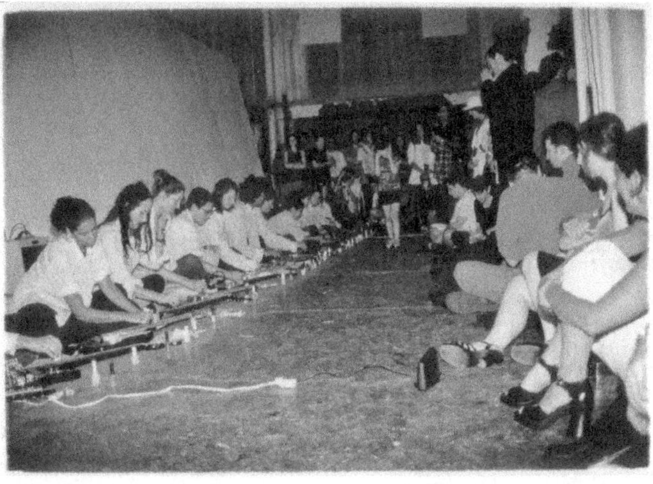

FIGURE 11 Marina Rosenfeld, *Sheer Frost Orchestra* at Greene Naftali Gallery, New York, 1997. Photographer unknown, courtesy of the artist.

gendered spaces of music creation that are inherent in all collective music-making. When this music is played in the gallery context, it is read differently than if this were performed either in a concert hall or in a rock venue, as the work slides into a critical zone rather than sitting squarely in a sound and music space. Here a group of women who may or may not know each other come together to learn to play an instrument they may not have previously touched and in doing so a space of learning together is created. 'In rehearsal, the women of the orchestra not only learn to play the piece; they are also transformed into the *Sheer Frost Orchestra*, complete with social, musical, and emotional bonds' (251).

In a way similar to *Sheer Frost Orchestra*, Rosenfeld works with young people for the piece *roygbiv&b*, originally performed at the Museum of Modern Art in 2011. The work employed a choir of young singers who sing mostly short melodies, which they begin out of time with each other. The effect in the hard-surfaced gallery was, as would be expected, a highly reverberant cloud of sound as one singer starts off and is swiftly joined by the choir. The gallery also houses a sound system created from large black horns and through which Rosenfeld plays electronic sounds. The work fully employed the hard surfaces and the open spaces of the atrium of the art museum, allowing the combination of electronic sounds, trombone, bass and the youth choir to reverberate throughout the adjoining gallery spaces.

Ari Benjamin Meyers, Marina Rosenfeld and Anri Sala have employed a range of non-mainstream music in their practice, including new music composition, Western art music and experimental music. However, the move to include music within the remit of contemporary art has not solely focused on 'serious' musical forms, as popular music has also become a focus. In these practices, musical forms that are widely recognized by the art-going public are exhibited, as well as music made by bands with a high public profile.

Paris-based Australian artist Angelica Mesiti produces highly polished film works that rely on well-known popular musical forms. She was originally a member of the King Pins, a performance and video installation group comprised four female artists, whose camp reproductions of rock songs sat as comfortably in the context of a drag show as it did in international biennales. Mesiti's subsequent solo career is preoccupied with themes of music and popular music culture, taking well-known popular songs or events and tweaking the context to provoke political or religious readings of everyday and popular music. She also uses music to make subtle politically charged artworks such as *Some dance to remember, some dance to forget* (2012), a video piece in which a partially blind musician performs a version of The Eagles's song 'Hotel California' on an electronic keyboard in a disco somewhere in Paris. The club is saturated in garish-coloured lights and the rendition of the song is poetic and strongly mesmerizing. The singer, Mohammed Lamourie, performs the song in the style of the Algerian fusion music called Raï, which has a political bent and usually contains lyrics concerned with social issues.

Mesiti's most recognized piece, *Rapture (silent anthem)* (2009), is based on footage of a large and young crowd dancing in front of a stage at the Big Day Out, an annual popular music festival. The audience is quintessentially white Australian in appearance – youthful, blonde and freckled. They watch their idols perform on a sunny summer's afternoon, their wide-eyed faces watching on in bliss. Mesiti filmed the crowd from under the stage in slow motion and the video is presented without sound. The lack of sound in this work draws our attention to the presence of sound in the event being documented. The sound emanating from these massive stages with an outdoor concert line-array sound system is brutally physical and the volume set at high decibel levels. Yet we do not hear what this youthful crowd hears – instead, we can only imagine the sonic experience. There is something spiritual or quasi-religious about the trance-like state these teens induced into by music, and that we witness. Writing on the work, Erika Kerruish describes the audience in the piece: 'Usually safely hidden in noise, speed and darkness, here they are stripped of sound and tempo and scrutinized, their euphoria thrown into relief. Within seemingly ordinary time and space, ecstatic experience is concealed' (2015, 593).

Mesiti's work shares its core concept with a psychedelic film piece by Ben Russell entitled *Black and White Trypps Number Three* (2007). This 35 mm film was shot during a performance by Lightning Bolt, a drums and bass duo from Providence, Rhode Island, known for their extremely noisy, lo-fi and fast-paced performances. In this film the stage is set by four minutes of the band playing at its usual frantic pace. At four minutes, the song at its usual pace finishes and the film and music transforms for the remaining seven and a half minutes into a spot-lit slow motion spectacle set to a slowed down drone sound edit of the original performance. The audience seems to slide into a state of drug-induced rapture, their eyes rolling back into their heads with sweat-covered faces and wet hair; they push and pull each other in the crowded space in front of the band.

Icelandic artist Ragnar Kjartansson (discussed in the previous chapter) uses music to explore well-known aspects of performance art, particularly extended duration and repetition. *The Visitors* (2012), shot at Rokeby Farm in upstate New York, is a sixty-two-minute piece in which a large band of musicians are recorded performing throughout its sprawling mansion. Kjartansson has said that he has 'always been interested in working with music as a visual art thing' (Kjartansson 2013). The nine-channel work follows a loosely assembled band of musicians who each perform in different rooms within the stately house. They play together, yet being in different parts of the house they must rely on headphones and ambient sound bleed to make a group performance. They are seen playing in various bedrooms, a large hall, the kitchen, a sitting room and a bathroom, with Kjartansson himself performing in a water-filled bathtub. The whole performance was recorded in one take to produce a nine-channel installation, this consisting of nine screens and nine mono speakers that each played back the audio and video of one of the individual performers. This allows the audience to engage with the individual performers and their sound when up close and, if moving towards the centre of the space, with the performers collectively, as the audio from the channels are combined into a single whole, akin in some ways to the experience of the original performance. Thus the audience can engage with the work as they desire, focusing on a single musician or finding sound combinations by moving around the gallery. *The Visitors* draws in its audience and directs them through the hour-long work using highly repetitive but engaging refrains and lyrics.

The work that in my view most strongly attests to the embrace of music within contemporary art occurred on the 5 May 2013 when Kjartansson employed American band, The National to perform their well-known song 'Sorrow' repeatedly for six straight hours at MoMA PS1 in New York. The performance was shot and edited into a six-hour-long single-channel, stereo video work entitled *A Lot of Sorrow* (2014). The work touches base with minimalist composition in its repetitive form and resembles a music documentary in which a concert is filmed in full; a very long documentary in this case. Seven performers dressed in black suits and white shirts line the stage in front of a sizeable audience. There is nothing out of the ordinary in this performance in terms of the band's appearance or the staging of the concert; this was not your typical art performance but simply an indie rock band performing a hit single. What was extraordinary, however, was the duration and the set-list. In the beginning of the recording we see a stagehand (Kjartansson himself) taping the set-list for the concert in front of the lead singer Matt Berninger, the list of course containing the same song title repeated over and over. In fact, the band performed the three-and-a-half-minute song one hundred and five times over the duration of the concert. The performance may be likened to Erik Satie's *Vexations* (1893) for which a single motif is performed continuously for 840 repetitions and takes some eighteen hours to perform. It also resonates with a myriad of durational performance art events, from Marina Abramović to Chris Burden. However, whereas extreme durational performance art is often about abstaining from the everyday, as is shown in the practice of an artist such as Tehching Hsieh who removed very basic life 'essentials' such as the freedom to move (away from one's house, or from someone else), the right to shelter and so on, *A Lot of Sorrow* is not about this kind of lack. The band members do not look nor act like performance artists and they are not abstaining from anything in particular. Like the audience they seem to be enjoying the experience, although it is an extreme one in many ways. What is undoubtedly different in relation from a more regular music concert is the fact that they are not playing a series of different songs played for the pleasure of the audience. Yet this audience knew the band would be performing only one song and they seem completely happy with this. In fact, the band performs one encore at the very end of the concert and the audience screams for the encore to be 'Sorrow', which of course it is.

I have discussed the installation of this work earlier, but it is important to briefly recap here as the work does not solely reside in the performance at MoMA PS1 nor its documentation and subsequent editing into a single-channelled video piece that more closely resembles an extended concert documentary than what we might expect of a video art work. The video runs for six hours, thus a single cycle of the work extends for approximately a full day's opening hours. Audiences invariably arrive some way into the performance and while The National play their song near perfectly every time, visitors experience very different parts of the performance depending on when they enter the space. Here the short three-and-a-half-minute music track is extended into a durational and highly repetitious artwork. Kjartansson has taken a highly recognizable song by a well-known indie rock band and through duration and repetition in a concert environment has turned the song into a durational piece of video art.

To end with a final example, Céleste Boursier-Mougenot's installation *From Here to Ear* (1999–) had been, at the time of writing, installed nineteen times in cities including Brisbane, Paris, London, New York and Montreal. The installation for the piece is particularly difficult in that it requires the transformation of the art gallery into an aviary to hold up to seventy zebra finches that in the course of the day 'play' electric guitars. They do this, unbeknown to them, by landing on the strings of horizontally installed electric guitars that are placed throughout the gallery. The sounds that are created within the installation are sporadic as the birds are so light that often landing on the strings does not create enough movement of the strings to produce any sound at all. Overall the sound is not dissimilar to a sparse indeterminate composition, with the sounds from lightly plucked guitar playing at random through guitar amplifiers placed around the perimeter of the gallery.

The purpose of this example is to draw attention one final time to both how sound is deeply embedded in the fabric of contemporary installation practice and how art galleries have become open to this practice, even when presented with highly demanding installation requirements. Boursier-Mougenot's work is complex to produce and to maintain as the birds have to be watched closely, with vets performing regular checks on the birds' well-being. Yet it has been installed continually since its premiere, and *From Here to Ear* has become one of the most recognizable installations of the early part of the century.

The receptiveness of the art institution to sound and in this case to sound through the context of music can also be witnessed in Kjartansson's *A Lot of Sorrow*, which has been shown regularly throughout the international art circuit since being produced, and like Boursier-Mougenot's installation, it asks a lot from the institution and its patrons. Yet both the exhibition and the artist have proved to be a draw card for audiences at major institutions as well as smaller art spaces. Furthermore, large-scale exhibitions such as Anri Sala: Answer Me point to the ability to produce audio intensive exhibitions and to the financial investment of the art institution in producing exhibitions that rely on an extensive audio component.

Artists who work with sound have come to be in high demand; many of those discussed in this book have high-profile careers, receiving survey shows, large installation commissions and places in important international biennales. Sala, Kjartansson and Boursier-Mougenot, alongside artists such as Cardiff and Fusinato, have spurred the development of the art gallery, such that in recent years the institutions have the knowledge and skills required to install sound with as much attention to detail as they have in installing object-based and visually orientated exhibitions. The conflict between the demand for sound in the gallery and the art institution that was historically heavily focused on visuality has made it very hard for the art institution to fully embrace sound, yet I am certain the art institution is coming to understand the importance of sound both within its bounds and within art itself in the last five to ten years.

Recently the new maturity in the relationship between the contemporary art world and sound was highlighted by a much-touted exhibition of 'sound art' entitled Soundings: A Contemporary Score, curated by Barbara London at MoMA in New York in 2013. This exhibition marks the symbolic end to the sound-themed art show. By sound-themed I mean the type of exhibition whose sole theme is simply 'sound' and in which the only thematic link between the exhibited works is that they all address or employ sound in some way. The build-up to Soundings was surrounded by much fanfare, so much so that the exhibition itself suffered under the weight of its own advertising spin. Bizarrely, the art museum in an attempt to stake a claim on what they believed to be the burgeoning field of 'sound art', framed Soundings as being, 'MoMA's first major exhibition of sound art'. This major art museum not only claimed to be presenting the first sound-themed exhibition within its art spaces but also by being the most recognized art museum in the world claimed by association the moment as its discovery.

Douglas Kahn has said numerous times that sound art is a field that keeps on being discovered: 'The term [sound art] was reinvigorated only when certain metropolitan art centers ... 'discovered' this thing called *sound art*. In London, it is supposed to have jumped off with the Hayward Gallery exhibition *Sonic Boom*' (2014, 335).

Sonic Boom was presented in 2000 and by then many large-scale events that put sound front and centre had already occurred, leading Kahn to argue that this so-called discovery was rather odd, especially given that Australia at that time was already 'onto its third generation of artists dealing with sound' (335). Thus the subsequent move by MoMA much later in 2013 was even more perplexing in its attempt to yet again discover sound-focused art, a move that, as it turns out, occurred too late to make any real impact, the sheer number of previous sound-themed exhibitions meant that Soundings had little chance of adding anything new to the 'sound in art' theme.

The claim that Soundings was a first was, however, factually incorrect, as Barbara London herself had curated an exhibition entitled Sound Art in 1979 at MoMA, an extremely progressive exhibition for its time, focusing solely on the work of three female artists: Connie Beckley, Julia Heyward and Maggie Payne. The claim of a first was also incorrect as there have been many sound-focused exhibitions within MoMA, it is just that those shows did not place 'sound' in their titles. Furthermore, London herself lists two such sound-focused exhibitions in the Soundings catalogue, namely Laurie Andersen's *Handphone Table* from 1978 and Terry Fox's *Room Temperature* from 1980 (London 2013, 15). It is worth noting that there was also a much earlier and more extensive exhibition that was also called Soundings, curated by Suzanne Delehanty in 1981 for the Neuberger Museum of Art in Purchase, New York State. This show was an early example of an exhibition that surveyed the sounding arts and subsequently many other sonically themed exhibitions have followed.

I would posit that sound-focused exhibitions have played an important role in shaping the developing art space in terms of the institution learning to work with a high number of sound-making art works and also by focusing the attention of art patrons towards thinking about art not simply as a visual practice but one that includes the senses beyond vision. However, by 2013, the audience for contemporary art was already well adjusted to hearing and understanding sonic practices within the frame of contemporary art, visiting contemporary art galleries with the expectation of having an art entertainment experience that more than likely will involve sound. As discussed in 'Noises in the Gallery', by the time the new millennium rolled around the audience attending art museums had substantially changed as the art entertainment industry developed much larger and louder art works, and the audience for contemporary art had actually developed into a much larger and noisier crowd than was expected in the middle of the twentieth century. Thus visitors to MoMA in 2013 would have expected that the museum's galleries would have been filled with art patrons and international tourists and that the galleries would already be a noisy and people-filled experience.

To this end, the art galleries exhibiting the audio intensive exhibitions of the artists discussed in this section have in the same timeframe not felt the compulsion to draw direct attention to the fact that these exhibitions include sound nor attempted to label them within the context of 'sound art'. Instead, the art spaces see these shows as exhibitions of work by the leading contemporary artists of the time and, while certainly pointing to sound and music within, there is no attempt to include 'sound' in the title nor place overt attention on the high level of production of audio as somehow exceptional or notable. That is, they not only do not apologize for the presence of audio by naming the work in the special category of 'sound art', but also critically enable a sonic understanding of these works by the very presence of sound and music as both theme and content of these installations.

What has been presented here in *Gallery Sound* suggests, ultimately, that sound has become enmeshed in contemporary art, and that the art institution has come to understand not only the importance of sound in art but also how to enable sound by installing it at a swiftly developing level of proficiency more akin to object-based and visual art works. Sound has taken a not inconsequential period of time to be embraced by the art institution, but after a slow start, sound integration into the art gallery is now so complete that it often does not even merit singling out. Through the inclusion and subsequent embrace of sound in contemporary art, our experience of the gallery arts is broadened and comes to be a much fuller and more human way of approaching galleries and the experience of art. If it is more human, it is because the conscious mobilization of sound in galleries is a gateway into reminding us of the range of ways we as humans can be influenced, affected and made aware of our surrounds through our senses.

NOTES

Introduction

1 While this book is focused on sound within the art space, there is room for future investigations of smell, touch and taste in this context.

2 Fusinato's work is here being used as an exemplar and the argument, I believe, can be directed towards any painting.

3 It should be noted here that deafness and other physical and psychological conditions might exclude some people from this comment, but it can also be noted that sound is not only sensed through the ear, it is also felt through the body via the vibrations created by sound waves.

4 The conference also raised questions about how to critique sound that was found in literary texts. Here words were used to draw out the sonic imagination of the reader that was then being reformed into further words, in the academic papers being presented, within the frame of the conference itself.

5 Klonk's term 'flexible art container' describes the gallery space built for the MoMA, one designed so that the walls and lighting could be moved and installed in different combinations for individual exhibitions. This allowed the exhibition designer and curator to restructure the space and direct the audience around the galleries in a deliberate manner. Klonk introduces this argument as a somewhat blunt critique of Brian O'Doherty's use of the term 'white cube' to describe modernist art gallery design. She asserts that the 'white cube' is formulated as an 'enclosed and isolated' container, rather than the flexible arrangement found at MoMA (Klonk 2009, 156). While this is the case for MoMA, there are many other situations where the cube is not so flexible.

6 I have discussed the term *sound art* most notably in *Cracked Media* (Kelly 2009, 16–17) and in the catalogue essay for *Sound Full: Sound in Contemporary Australian and New Zealand Art* (Kelly 2013, 11).

Chapter 1

1 For a discussion of the Art and Technology Program, see Kahn (2012).

2 See Nauman's Catalogue Raisonne (Benezra, Halbreich and Simon 1994).

3 Bruce Nauman, letter to Konrad Fischer dated 22 January 1970. Dorothee and Konrad Fischer Archive.

4 It is important to note that many of the works from this period are quoted as having quite different names in the literature. For this chapter I have used the Catalogue Raisonne as the point of reference in terms of naming conventions for these works (Benezra, Halbreich and Simon 1994).

5 Nauman, in a letter dated 3 January 1970, gives Konrad Fischer instructions on how to fabricate the wall, making it clear that the material on the outside is there only to hold in the fibreglass sound-dampening material. This was reiterated in a letter dated 22 January. Also in this letter Nauman discusses works with fans and the acoustic experience generated by the air being moved around the space.

6 For a broader discussion of Paik's *Random Access* within the frame of cracked media, see Kelly (2009, 135–9).

7 In spite of the similarity between the work and Conrad's own method, such confluence would appear to be merely coincidental, for it would seem unlikely that Nauman could have experienced a Conrad performance at this time, and Conrad himself did not recollect having heard of or having met Nauman in this period. For his part, Conrad heard Nauman's work as being quite different from his own, since Conrad's 'use of beat rhythms is always related to a (virtual) harmonic fundamental pitch a number of octaves below the sounding tones' (Conrad 2014).

8 In Jeremy Grimshaw's description of minding the *Dream House*, he recounts that at the end of the day the faders on the mixing desk were simply lowered; thus the work was not turned off, it was just turned down (Grimshaw 2011, 122).

9 The durations that audience members stayed are based on my own observation of being in the gallery for a period of one hour.

10 Note *I am Sitting in a Room* is often dated 1970, but the composition was actually created and first recorded in 1969. It had its first performance in 1970 and this is most likely the reason for it being dated 1970.

11 See 'Musical Galleries' for more on the use of the art gallery for musical performance.

Chapter 2

1 http://tate.org.uk (no longer available online).

2 In 2015 a new sponsor, Hyundai, was engaged for a new series of commissions.

3 It should be noted that subsequently overtly political installations have been staged in the Turbine Hall, not least of which was Ai Weiwei's *Sunflower Seeds* in 2010.

4 The Tate Modern opened two new extensions in 2016, The Tanks and The Switch House. The former is located within the powerhouse's oil tanks and the latter is a large tower built on the site of the original switch house. The Tanks extension provides space specifically for live art and is another example of refurbishment of industrial architecture for use by the art museum.

5 An image from the documentation of Kusum Normoyle's performance for the opening of Sound Full appears on the cover of this book.

6 See http://www.santiago-sierra.com/200014_1024.php (accessed 22 October 2015).

7 Ragnar Kjartansson's *A Lot of Sorrow* will be further discussed in the later section 'Music as Art'.

8 For a broader discussion of Schafer's conceptualization of the soundscape, see Kelman (2010, 212–34).

9 See Douglas Kahn's discussion of Christina Kubisch's work within a wider examination of the electromagnetic arts in his book *Earth Sound, Earth Signal* (Kahn 2013, 239–40).

Chapter 3

1 One particular performance of Reich's *Four Organs* by the Boston Symphony at Carnegie Hall in 1973 is a case in point, as *New York Times* critic Harold C. Schonberg described the scene as if 'red-hot needles were being inserted under fingernails' of the audience (Schonberg 1973).

2 See Thompson (2002).

3 Reich had been involved with the Park Place Gallery where he held earlier concerts and collaborated with artists and musicians. He had also been in a group show at the gallery entitled Fleming / Ross / Foyster / Reich in the spring of 1967. Reich's role in this exhibition was, as could be expected, sound-based. His composition *Melodica* (1966) played in the gallery on continuous loop (Chapman 2013, 34–5).

4 See the impermanent.audio archive: http://impermanent.info.

BIBLIOGRAPHY

Art21. 2001. 'Bruce Nauman: Setting a Good Corner'. In *Art in the Twenty-First Century*.

Asher, Michael. 1983. *Writings 1973-1983 on Works 1969-1979*. Edited by B. H. D. Buchloh. Halifax, NS: Press of the Nova Scotia College of Art and Design and the Museum of Contemporary Art Los Angeles.

Augoyard, Jean-François. 2007. *Step by Step: Everyday Walks in a French Urban Housing Project*. Minneapolis: University of Minnesota Press.

Auping, Michael. 2011. 'Stealth Architecture: Rooms of Light and Space'. In *Phenomenal: California Light, Space, Surface*, edited by Robin Clark, 79–104. Berkeley: University of California Press.

Benezra, Neal, Kathy Halbreich and Joan Simon, ed. 1994. *Bruce Nauman: Exhibition Catalogue and Catalogue Raisonné*. Minneapolis: Walker Art Center.

Blackson, Robert. Email message to author, 29 June 2016.

Blamey, Peter. 2008. 'Sine Waves and Simple Acoustic Phenomena in Experimental Music – with Special Reference to the Work of La Monte Young and Alvin Lucier'. PhD, University of Western Sydney.

Blesser, Barry, and Linda-Ruth Salter. 2007. *Spaces Speak, Are You Listening?: Experiencing Aural Architecture*. Cambridge, MA: MIT Press.

Bull, Michael. 2005. 'No Dead Air! The iPod and the Culture of Mobile Listening'. *Leisure Studies* 24 (4): 343–55.

Bull, Michael. 2007. *Sound Moves: iPod Culture and Urban Experience*. London and New York: Routledge.

Butterfield, Jan. 2003. 'Bruce Nauman: The Center of Yourself (1975)'. In *Please Pay Attention Please: Bruce Nauman's Words*, edited by Janet Kraynak, 173–82. Cambridge, MA: MIT Press.

Cage, John. 1967. *A Year From Monday: New Lectures and Writings*. Middletown, CT: Wesleyan University Press.

Cardiff, Janet. 1997. 'Chiaroscuro'. Accessed 27 October 2015. http://www.cardiffmiller.com/artworks/walks/chiaroscuro.html.

Cardiff, Janet. 2001. 'Pleasure Principals: The Art of Janet Cardiff and George Bures Miller' – from an Interview. *Border Crossings* 78.

Accessed 19 February. http://bordercrossingsmag.com/article/pleasure-principals-the-art-of-janet-cardiff-and-george-bures-miller.

Carlson, Marla. 2006. 'Looking, Listening, and Remembering: Ways to Walk New York after 9/11'. *Theatre Journal* 58 (3): 395–416.

Celant, Germano. 1975. 'Artspace'. *Studio International* 190 (977): 115–23.

Chapman, David Allen. 2013. 'Collaboration, Presence, and Community: The Philip Glass Ensemble in Downtown New York, 1966–1976'. PhD, Washington University in St. Louis.

Cole, Ross. 2014. '"Sound Effects (O.K., Music)": Steve Reich and the Visual Arts in New York City, 1966-1968'. *Twentieth-Century Music* 11 (2): 217–44.

Connor, Steven. 2011. 'Ears Have Walls: On Hearing Art'. In *Sound*, edited by Caleb Kelly, 129–39. London and Cambridge, MA: Whitechapel Gallery/MIT Press.

Connor, Steven. 2015. 'Acousmania'. *Sound Studies: Art, Experience, Politics Conference, The University of Cambridge*. Accessed 13 November 2016. http://stevenconnor.com/acousmania.html.

Conrad, Tony. Email correspondence with the author, 16 October 2014.

Copeland, Mathieu, ed. 2009. *Voids: A Retrospective*. Paris: Éditions du Centre Pompidou and Centre Pompidou-Metz.

Davidts, Wouter. 2006. 'Art Factories: Museums of Contemporary Art and the Promise of Artistic Production, from Centre Pompidou to Tate Modern'. *Fabrications* 16 (1): 23–42.

Davidts, Wouter. 2008. 'The Vast and the Void. On Tate Modern's Turbine Hall and The Unilever Series'. *Footprint* 1 (1): 77–92.

Dexter, Emma. 2005. 'Raw Materials'. In *Bruce Nauman: Raw Materials*, 18–23. London: Tate Publishing.

Drobnick, Jim. 1995. 'Mock Excursions and Twisted Itineraries: Tour Guide Performances'. *Parachute* 80 (October/December): 31–7.

Egoyan, Atom. 2002. 'Janet Cardiff'. *BOMB* 79 (Spring): 60–7.

Eidsheim, Nina Sun. 2015. *Sensing Sound: Singing & Listening As Vibrational Practice, Sign, Storage, Transmission*. Durham: Duke University Press.

Fisher, Jennifer. 1999. 'Speeches of Display: The Museum Audioguides of Sophie Callie, Andrea Fraser and Janet Cardiff'. *Parachute: Contemporary Art* 94 (April–June): 25–31.

Fraser, Andrea. 1997. 'What's Intangible, Transitory, Mediating, Participatory, and Rendered in the Public Sphere?' *October* 80: 111–16.

Fusinato, Marco. 2009. 'Double Infinitives'. Accessed 17 August 2016. http://marcofusinato.com/art/double-infinitives/.

Fusinato, Marco. 2015. 'Marco Fusinato 13 Questions'. Accessed 20 February 2017. http://preparedguitar.blogspot.com.au/2015/02/marco-fusinato-13-questions.html.

Garver, Tomas H. 1970. 'Michael Asher at La Jolla Art Museum'. *Artforum* 8 (5): 75–6.

Graham, Dan. 1993. *Rock My Religion, 1965-1990*. Cambridge, MA: MIT Press.

Greenberg, Reesa. 1996. 'The Exhibited Redistributed: A Case for Reassessing Space'. In *Thinking About Exhibitions*, edited by Reesa Greenberg, Bruce W. Ferguson and Sandy Nairne, 246–58. New York: Routledge.

Grimshaw, Jeremy. 2011. *Draw a Straight Line and Follow it: The Music and Mysticism of La Monte Young*. New York: Oxford University Press.

Hainge, Greg. 2013. *Noise Matters: Towards an Ontology of Noise*. New York: Bloomsbury Academic.

Hatanaka, Minoru. 2002–2003. 'From an "Off" Site: Off Site and the Sounds Produced There'. *Improvised Music From Japan* (1): 8–11.

Hegarty, Paul. 2001. 'Full with Noise: Theory and Japanese Noise Music'. *Ctheory*. Accessed 19 February 2017. http://www.ctheory.net/text_file.asp?pick=314.

Hegarty, Paul. 2007. *Noise/Music: A History*. New York: Continuum.

Ingold, Tim. 2000. *The Perception of the Environment: Essays on Livelihood, Dwelling and Skill*. London: Routledge.

Ingold, Tim. 2008. 'Against Soundscape'. In *Autumn Leaves: Sound and the Environment in Artistic Practice*, edited by Angus Carlyle, 10–13. Paris: Double Entendre Paris.

Ingold, Tim. 2011. 'Worlds of Sense and Sensing the World: A Response to Sarah Pink and David Howes.' *Social Anthropology* 19 (3): 313–17.

Jackson, Shannon. 2011. *Social Works: Performing Art, Supporting Publics*. New York: Routledge.

Joseph, Branden W. 2008. *Beyond the Dream Syndicate: Tony Conrad and the arts after Cage*. New York: Zone Books.

Joseph, Branden W. 2011. 'Dark Energy: The Art of Marco Fusinato'. *Artforum* 49 (6): 192–9.

Joseph, Branden W. 2014. 'The Shard in the Wound'. In *Marco Fusinato: Let's Destroy Work*, edited by Marco Fusinato. Melbourne: Schwartz City.

Kahn, Douglas. 1990. 'Audio Art in the Deaf Century'. In *Sound by Artists*, edited by Dan Lander and Micah Lexier, 301–29. Toronto: Art Metropole.

Kahn, Douglas. 1999. *Noise, Water, Meat: A History of Sound in the Arts*. Cambridge, MA: MIT Press.

Kahn, Douglas. 2012. 'The Military-Arts Nexus: Two cases in the United States, c. 1970'. *Studies in Material Thinking* 8.

Kahn, Douglas. 2013. *Earth Sound Earth Signal: Energies and Earth Magnitude in the Arts*. Berkeley: University of California Press.

Kahn, Douglas. 2014. 'Sound Art, Art, Music'. *Tacet* 3: 329–47.
Kelly, Caleb. 2009. *Cracked Media: The Sound of Malfunction*. Cambridge, MA: MIT Press.
Kelly, Caleb. 2013. *Sound Full: Sound in Contemporary Australian and New Zealand Art*. Dunedin: Dunedin Public Art Gallery.
Kelman, Ari. 2010. 'Rethinking the Soundscape'. *Senses and Society* 5 (2): 212–34.
Kennedy, Chris. 2013. 'Akio Suzuki: Stop and Listen to the World'. *Musicworks* 115. Accessed 20 February 2017. https://www.musicworks.ca/featured-article/featured-article/akio-suzuki.
Kerruish, Erika. 2015. 'Angelica Mesiti's Rapture (Silent Anthem): Hearing With Our Eyes'. *Continuum* 29 (4): 593–604. Doi: 10.1080/10304312.2015.1025365.
Kim-Cohen, Seth. 2009. *In the Blink of an Ear: Towards a Non-Cochlear Sonic Art*. New York: Continuum.
Kjartansson, Ragnar. 2013. 'The Visitors'. Accessed 31 July 2016. Pirelli HangarBicocca. https://www.youtube.com/watch?v=lcwGnWuXJuU.
Klonk, Charlotte. 2009. *Spaces of Experience: Art Gallery Interiors From 1800 to 2000*. New Haven: Yale University Press.
Kraynak, Janet. 2003. 'Dependent Participation: Bruce Nauman's Environments'. *Grey Room* (10): 22–45.
Kraynak, Janet. 2014. *Nauman Reiterated*. Minneapolis: University of Minnesota Press.
Kriegsman, Alan. 1969. 'Ecstacy'. *The Washington Post*, 30 May.
LaBelle, Brandon. 2006. *Background Noise: Perspectives on Sound Art*. New York: Continuum.
Licht, Alan. 2007. *Sound Art: Beyond Music, Between Categories*. New York: Rizzoli.
Lippard, Lucy, and John Chandler. 1971. 'The Dematerialization of Art'. In *Changing: Essays in Art Criticism*, edited by Lucy Lippard, 46–50. New York: Dutton.
Lippard, Lucy R. 1973. *Six Years: The Dematerialization of the Art Object From 1966 to 1972; A Cross-Reference Book of Information on Some Esthetic Boundaries*. New York: Praeger.
London, Barbera. 2013. 'Soundings: From the 1960s to the Present Barbara London'. In *Soundings: A Contemporary Score*, 8–15. New York: The Museum of Modern Art.
López, Francisco. 2004. 'Against the Stage'. Accessed 28 July 2016. http://www.franciscolopez.net/stage.html.
Lucier, Alvin. 1995. *Reflections: Interviews, Scores, Writings*. Köln: Musik Texte.
Lucier, Alvin. 2012. *Music 109: Notes on Experimental Music*. Middletown, CT: Wesleyan University Press.

Marioni, Tom. 1970. 'MOCA/FM: Sound Sculpture As'. https://archive.org/details/MFM_1970_04_30_c1.

Masséra, Jean-Charles. 2002. 'Dance With the Law'. In *Bruce Nauman*, edited by Robert C. Morgan, 174–88. Baltimore: Johns Hopkins University Press.

Meyer, James. 2004. 'No More Scale: The Experience of Size in Contemporary Sculpture'. *Artforum* 42 (10): 220–8.

Meyers, Ari Benjamin. 2013. 'Music as an Art Form: A Conversation Between Anri Sala and Ari Benjamin Meyers'. *ArtMag* 76. Accessed 20 February 2017. http://db-artmag.com/en/76/feature/music-as-an-art-form-a-conversation-between-anri-sala-and-ari-be/.

Microsoft. 2015. 'The World's Quietist Place'. Accessed 17 August 2016. http://news.microsoft.com/stories/building87/audio-lab.php.

Migone, Christof. 2012. *Sonic Somatic: Performances of the Unsound Body*. Berlin: Errant Bodies Press.

Moles, Kate, and Angharad Saunders. 2015. 'Ragged Places and Smooth Surfaces: Audio Walks as Practices of Making and Doing the City'. *Journal of Urban Cultural Studies* 2 (1+2): 151–64.

Monte, James. 1969. 'Anti-Illusion: Procedures/Materials'. In *Anti-Illusion: Procedures/Materials*, 4–23. New York: Whitney Museum of American Art.

Moore, Carman. 1966. 'Park Place Electronics'. *Village Voice* (9): 17.

Morton, Timothy. 2007. *Ecology Without Nature: Rethinking Environmental Aesthetics*. Cambridge, MA: Harvard University Press.

Myers, Misha. 2011. 'Vocal Landscaping: The Theatre of Sound in Audiowalks'. In *Theatre Noise: The Sound of Performance*, edited by Lynne Kendrick and David Roesner, 70–81. Newcastle: Cambridge Scholars.

Nedelkopoulou, Eirini. 2011. 'Walking Out on Our Bodies Participation as Ecstasis in Janet Cardiff's Walks'. *Performance Research* 16 (4): 117–23.

Nyman, Michael. 1976. 'Steve Reich: Interview'. *Studio International* 192 (984): 300–7.

O'Doherty, Brian. 1999. *Inside the White Cube: The Ideology of the Gallery Space*. Berkeley: University of California Press.

Ouzounian, Gascia. 2015. 'Sound Installation Art: From Spatial Poetics to Politics, Aesthetics to Ethics'. In *Music, Sound and Space Transformations of Public and Private Experience*, edited by Georgina Born, 73–89. Cambridge: Cambridge University Press.

Peltomäki, Kirsi. 2010. *Situation Aesthetics: The Work of Michael Asher*. Cambridge, MA: MIT Press.

Peltomäki, Kirsi. 2014. 'Outside the Walls: Navigating the Sensory in Michael Asher's Situations'. *Tacet* 3: 47–66.

Prior, Nick. 2003. 'Having One's Tate and Eating It: Transformations of the Museum in a Hypermodern Era'. In *Art and its Publics: Museum Studies at the Millennium*, edited by Andrew McClellan, 51–76. Malden, MA: Blackwell Pub. Co.

Ratcliff, Carter. 1970. 'New York Letter'. *Art International* 14 (2): 77–80.

Reich, Steve. 2000. 'Steve Reich on "Pendulum Music"'. Accessed 21 April 2016. http://www.furious.com/perfect/ohm/reich.html.

Rockwell, John. 1973. 'Sound of New Music is Likened to Art'. *New York Times*, 3 January, 48.

Rosenfeld, Marina. 2002. 'The Sheer Frost Orchestra: A Nail Polish Bottle, A Guitar String and the Birth of an Orchestra'. *Leonardo Music Journal* 12 (1): 59–61.

Ross, Christine. 2013. 'Movement That Matters Historically: Janet Cardiff and George Bures Miller's 2012 *Alter Bahnhof Video Walk*'. *Discourse* 35 (2): 212–27.

Sala, Anri. 2013. 'Music as an Art Form: A Conversation between Anri Sala and Ari Benjamin Meyers'. *ArtMag* 76. http://db-artmag.com/en/76/feature/music-as-an-art-form-a-conversation-between-anri-sala-and-ari-be/.

Sala, Anri, and Massimiliano Gioni. 2016. 'Guided by Voices, Lured by Sounds: An Interview'. In *Anri Sala: Answer Me*, edited by Margot Norton and Massimiliano Gioni, 80–97. New York: New Museum & Phaidon.

Schafer, R. Murray. 1993. *The Soundscape: Our Sonic Environment and the Tuning of the World*. Rochester, VT: Destiny Books.

Schonberg, Harold C. 1973. 'Music: A Concert Fuss'. *New York Times*, 20 January, 36. http://www.nytimes.com/1973/01/20/archives/music-a-concert-fuss-piece-by-reich-draws-a-vocal-reaction-the.html?_r=0.

Schuld, Dawna. 2010. 'Lost in Space: Consciousness and Experiment in the Work of Irwin and Turrell'. In *Beyond Mimesis and Convention: Representation in Art and Science*, edited by Roman Frigg and Matthew C. Hunter, 221–44. New York: Springer.

Schuld, Dawna. 2011. 'Practically Nothing: Light, Space, and the Pragmatics of Phenomenology'. In *Phenomenal: California Light, Space, Surface*, edited by Robin Clark, 105–22. Berkeley: University of California Press.

Schulze, Holger. 2013. 'The Corporeality of Listening. Experiencing Soundscapes on Audio Guides'. In *Soundscapes of the Urban Past*, edited by Karin Bijsterveld, 195–208. Bielefeld: Transcript.

Serra, Richard, and Clara Weyergraf. 1980. *Richard Serra, Interviews, etc., 1970-1980*. Yonkers, NY: Archer Fields Pr.

Sharp, Willoughby. 2003a. 'Interview with Bruce Nauman (1971)'. In *Please Pay Attention Please: Bruce Nauman's Words*, edited by Janet Kraynak, 133–54. Cambridge, MA: MIT Press.

Sharp, Willoughby 2003b. 'Nauman Interview (1970)'. In *Please Pay Attention Please: Bruce Nauman's Words*, edited by Janet Kraynak, 111–32. Cambridge, MA: MIT Press.

Shaviro, Steven. 2011. 'Bilinda Butcher'. In *Sound*, edited by Caleb Kelly, 120–3. London and Cambridge, MA: Whitechapel Gallery/MIT Press. Original edition, Shaviro, Steven, *Doom Patrols: A Theoretical Fiction About Postmodernism*. London: High Risk Books, 1997.

Simon, Joan. 2003. 'Breaking the Silence: An Interview with Bruce Nauman (January 1987)'. In *Please Pay Attention Please: Bruce Nauman's Words*, edited by Janet Kraynak, 317–38. Cambridge, MA: MIT Press.

Simon, Joan. 2004. 'Hear, Hear: An Interview with Bruce Nauman'. *Frieze* 86: 130–37.

Springgay, Stephanie, ed. 2012. *Diane Borsato*. Toronto: Art Gallery of York University.

Sterne, Jonathan. 2003. *The Audible Past: Cultural Origins of Sound Reproduction*. Durham: Duke University Press.

Stone, Rob. 2015. *Auditions: Architecture and Aurality*. Cambridge, MA: MIT Press.

Suzuki, Akio. 2012. *Akio Suzuki with Aki Onda*. Accessed 16 February 2017. http://issueprojectroom.org/news/akio-suzuki-aki-onda.

Tallon, Loïc. 2008. 'Introduction: Mobile, Digital, and Personal'. In *Digital Technologies and the Museum Experience: Handheld Guides and Other Media*, edited by Loïc Tallon and Kevin Walker, xiii–xxv. Lanham: AltaMira Press.

Thompson, Emily Ann. 2002. *The Soundscape of Modernity: Architectural Acoustics and the Culture of Listening in America, 1900-1933*. Cambridge, MA: MIT Press.

Tubridy, Derval. 2007. 'Sounding Spaces Aurality in Samuel Beckett, Janet Cardiff and Bruce Nauman'. *Performance Research* 12 (1): 5–11.

Tuchman, Maurice. 1971. *A Report on the Art and Technology Program of the Los Angeles County Museum of Art. 1967-1971*. New York: Viking.

Tucker, Marcia. 1969. 'Anti-Illusion: Procedures/Materials'. In *Anti-Illusion: Procedures/Materials*, 24–44. New York: Whitney Museum of American Art.

Tucker, Marcia. 1970. 'PheNAUMANology'. *Artforum* 9 (4): 38–44.

Tucker, Marcia, and Liza Lou. 2008. *A Short Life of Trouble: Forty Years in the New York Art World*. Berkeley: University of California Press.

Uroskie, Andrew V. 2014. *Between the Black Box and the White Cube: Expanded Cinema and Postwar Art*. Chicago: University of Chicago Press.

Van Bruggen, Coosje. 1988. *Bruce Nauman*. New York: Rizzoli.

Van Bruggen, Coosje. 2002. 'Sounddance: Bruce Nauman'. In *Bruce Nauman*, edited by Robert C. Morgan, 43–69. Baltimore: Johns Hopkins University Press.

Wasserman, Emily. 1969. 'Process, Whitney Museum'. *Artforum* 8 (1): 57–8.

Weschler, Lawrence, and Robert Irwin. 1982. *Seeing is Forgetting the Name of the Thing One Sees: A Life of Contemporary Artist Robert Irwin*. Berkeley: University of California Press.

Young, La Monte. 1965. 'Lecture 1960'. *The Tulane Drama Review* 10 (2): 73–83.

Young, La Monte, and Marian Zazeela. 1996. 'Continuous Sound and Light Environments'. In *Sound and Light: La Monte Young and Marian Zazeela*, edited by William Duckworth and Richard Fleming, 218–21. Lewisberg: Bucknell University Press.

INDEX

Page numbers in italics refer to figures